Home Workshops

W9-CES-638

Created and Designed by the Editorial Staff of Ortho Books

Project Editor
Norm Rae

Writers
William Bigelow
Maureen Bigelow

Principal Photographer
Kenneth Rice

Illustrators
Glenn Cavalli
Edith Allgood

Ortho Books

Publisher
Richard E. Pile, Jr.

Editorial Director
Christine Jordan

Production Director
Ernie S. Tasaki

Managing Editors
Robert J. Beckstrom
Michael D. Smith
Sally W. Smith

System Manager
Linda M. Bouchard

Marketing Administrative Assistant
Daniel Stage

Distribution Specialist
Barbara F. Steadham

Sales Manager
Thomas J. Leahy

Technical Consultant
J. A. Crozier, Jr., Ph.D.

Copy Chief
Melinda E. Levine

Editorial Coordinator
Cass Dempsey

Copyeditor
Irene Elmer

Proofreader
Deborah Bruner

Indexer
Trisha Feuerstein

Editorial Assistants
John Parr
Nancy Patton Wilson

Composition by
Laurie A. Steele

Layout & Production by
Studio 165

Separations by
Color Tech Corp.

Lithographed in the USA by
Webcrafters, Inc.

Photographers
With the exception of the following, all photographs in this book are by Kenneth Rice. Names of photographers are followed by the page numbers on which their work appears.
R = right, C = center,
L = left, T = top, B = bottom.

John Birchard: 28, 34, 64, 65, 87
Fred Lyon: 13TR
Deborah Porter: 24, 34, 65, 72, 78, 84, 86
Norm Rae: 88, 92, 93

Special Thanks To
Fernando Aguayo
Bob Berryman
Bill Bitz
John Bocks
Mike Brady
Doug Cooper
Doug Keck
Clarence Kellog
Glenn Krueg
Jim Lorette
Tom McPhadden
Fred Socher
Bob Stocksdale
George Thompson
Paul Waterman

Permission to use the design of the sanding bench on page 20 is granted by *Popular Woodworking* magazine.

NOTE: Some photographs show shop tools with blade guards removed for photographic purposes. Never operate power shop tools without proper safety precautions.

Front Cover
Well-planned and organized, this shop in a converted two-car garage has plenty of work and storage space.

Title Page
This converted pool house with its double glass doors is an inviting and roomy home workshop.

Page 3
This unique drill-bit storage arrangement is a good example of a planned and organized work space in a home workshop.

Back Cover
Top left: This converted pool house makes a roomy and airy home workshop.
Top right: A well-organized portable tool chest can bring the shop to the project.
Bottom left: Machinery on wheels transforms limited space into an efficient workshop.
Bottom right: Identifying hardware is made easy when samples are fastened to each drawer.

SURFORM is a registered trademark of Stanley Power Tools.

No portion of this book may be reproduced without written permission from the publisher.

We are not responsible for unsolicited manuscripts, photographs, or illustrations.

Before purchasing materials discussed in this book, be sure to check with local building authorities to verify and review all construction steps.

Every effort has been made at the time of publication to guarantee the accuracy of the names and addresses of information sources and suppliers, and in the technical data and recommendations contained. However, readers should check for their own assurance and must be responsible for selection and use of suppliers, supplies, materials, and chemical products.

Address all inquiries to:
Ortho Books
Chevron Chemical Company
Consumer Products Division
Box 5047
San Ramon, CA 94583-0947

Copyright © 1992
Chevron Chemical Company
All rights reserved under international and Pan-American copyright conventions.

1 2 3 4 5 6 7 8 9
92 93 94 95 96 97 98

ISBN 0-89721-239-8
Library of Congress Catalog Card
Number 91-73778

Chevron

Chevron Chemical Company
6001 Bollinger Canyon Road, San Ramon, CA 94583

Home Workshops

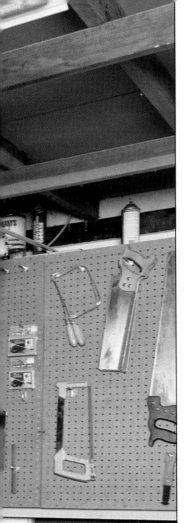

PLANNING A HOME WORKSHOP

It takes planning to create a home workshop. First, you must define your needs. Where will the new workshop be located? What tools will it contain? How much money do you have to spend? In addition, you should plan for future expansion—some day you may need more tools and more work space.

This book will help you to reorganize existing spaces in your home to create everything from a tiny closet workshop to a master handicrafter's dream shop. It shows how to build the best shop for your space and budget. It covers storage, lighting, ventilation, electrical power, space requirements, noise reduction, and safety tips. It also covers the choice and use of various kinds of tools.

Ample storage, easy access to tools, and space to move around in show that the workshop in this converted two-car garage was well planned and organized.

THE SPACES IN YOUR HOME

The typical home offers many possible locations for a workshop. Think about potential spaces now, but don't choose one until you have read the entire book. It will help you evaluate all of the issues that will affect your choices.

Small and Large Spaces

Small spaces challenge your ingenuity. If you live in a small house or in an apartment, think about all of the possible corners where a home workshop could be fitted in. If you are fortunate enough to have a larger space at your disposal, you must still use ingenuity and planning to achieve your goals.

A Kitchen Corner

A corner in the kitchen can provide the space for a small shop area. Cupboards that are too deep for daily use can be excellent for storing a few power tools. Most kitchens have sturdy countertops that can double as workbenches. There are usually several convenient electrical outlets, and the lighting in modern kitchens is designed to provide illumination for close work. Water is available for cleanup. The exhaust fan over the stove can provide adequate ventilation if it vents to the outdoors.

Because the kitchen is also used for other household activities, you should determine the high-traffic areas in order to avoid conflicts. Draw a sketch of the kitchen, including the proposed workshop, on graph paper. Include all areas of activity that would be near the workshop space. Consider all the uses of the kitchen and decide whether a small workshop can be made to fit in.

A Piece of Furniture

Do you have an old desk or a bureau stored in the attic or cluttering up a corner of the hall? Such pieces of furniture can make excellent small workshops. The drawers, especially ones with dividers, can be used to store tools and parts, and the top can function as a work surface. These made-over pieces needn't be ugly; refinished with fresh paint or stain, they can add beauty and charm to your home. The secret of the shop-in-a-bureau is that it looks like one thing when it is actually another. If you don't have any pieces of unused furniture, check the classified section of the local newspaper for garage sales. You may find just what you need at very little cost.

A Space Beneath the Stairs

The space under a flight of stairs is usually wasted. Perhaps now is the time to change that space into an efficient workshop. If the stairs are on an upper floor, weight is an important consideration. Will your tools, workbench, and anticipated projects be heavy enough to put too much stress on the floor and potentially weaken any supports? Consider too the task of carrying tools and supplies upstairs and the effect that noise and fumes will have on the occupants of adjacent rooms. A better place would be underneath the basement staircase.

An Empty Closet

An unused closet makes a fine home workshop. A double-sized or walk-in closet is ideal, but any closet has wall space and shelves that can be used for tool storage. Think carefully about the closet that you choose. Remember that household traffic patterns will affect the use of certain closets. Again, if the closet is on an upper floor, you must consider access, weight, and noise. Another very important consideration for a closet workshop is ventilation.

A Spare Room

A dream shop could be built in an unused room. It has lots of wall space, windows, and often a closet that can be used for tool storage. It has plenty of work space, and it provides convenient access to tools. Its location within the house is important. A first-floor room containing a closet and several electrical outlets would be ideal. A room on an upper floor is less desirable for all of the reasons previously cited. Bear in mind too that some power tools will cause the floor and the downstairs ceiling to vibrate.

The Attic

Most attics are used for storage, but with planning and organizing an attic may accommodate a workshop as well. Headroom is an important factor. You will probably want to place the workbench in the center of the attic and build in storage along the sides, where the angle of the roof will not allow you to stand upright. Ventilation, heating, and cooling are important too; the space must be well ventilated and must feel comfortable all year around. Again, consider access. Will it be convenient to move tools and materials in and out? In general, an attic space is more suitable for a small shop oriented to crafts, jewelry, clock repair, and so forth than it is to a large woodshop, for example.

The Garage

The garage is as traditional a location for a workshop as it is for the family car. Because

Spaces in the Home

garages are usually well ventilated and well lit, garage space can be turned into an ideal shop. Since the garage is ordinarily used for many different purposes, you will need to install metal cabinets with locks for storing tools and toxic substances. Usually the electrical system is adequate, but outlets can easily be added to the open studded walls if necessary. You may need to provide heat.

The Basement

People that live in houses with basements have been going downstairs to work on projects for years. Like the garage, the basement is a traditional location for a workshop. There is usually plenty of room for a workbench and floor-standing power tools. In addition, the basement is usually cool in the summer, and because the furnace is located there, warm in the winter.

A Shed

If you can't fit a workshop into the house or garage, consider erecting a prefabricated shed. These sheds are made of metal or wood and can be purchased complete or in kit form. Choose one that harmonizes with the style of the house. The size should be appropriate to the location, which should provide easy access but should not interfere with the use of the yard.

The building code specifies the distance that a freestanding building can be placed from a shared property line. Consult those local officials who are responsible for enforcing building codes for more information.

A Barn

Barns provide the largest space for a home workshop. Some barns have doors on either end that make it easy to move materials and projects in and out. A three-car garage offers similar ease of access. The proper use of such abundant space should be planned as carefully as you would plan the smallest home workshop.

A Mobile or Portable Shop

Have tools, will travel may be your motto. Even in the house some jobs demand a portable set of tools. Toilets and sinks don't come to us, and woodworkers cannot always bring their work into the shop. A portable workbench or a tool caddy comes in handy when repair projects take you to different parts of the house.

DEVELOPING THE PLAN

By now you may have some idea where you'd like to install the new workshop. Don't immediately set up the workbench there; plan first. This spot will be yours for a long time, so make sure that it is the right one. You might want to keep two or three alternate locations in mind. As you plan, you can narrow them down to the best all-around choice.

The Focus of the Workshop

The design of the shop will be affected by its focus—crafts, mechanical or electrical work, woodworking, or general home repair. Visualize all of the operations that you will be carrying out in the new shop. For example, a woodworking shop might require a workbench, a machining area, tool storage, and a finishing area. In a larger shop the machining area must be divided into spaces for cutting and planing large pieces of lumber and spaces for finish cutting, drilling, routing, and sanding.

Draw a Floor Plan

On a piece of graph paper, draw a general floor plan; include lights, doorways, outlets, and windows. Draw shapes that represent benches and stationary power tools. On other pieces of graph paper, make elevation drawings of the walls, showing where you would place the shelves and cabinets. Draw each wall on a separate piece of paper. The length of the wall is the length of the floor, and the height is the height of the ceiling. Include windows, doors, and all the potential bench and storage areas. Write in the dimensions of the windows, doors, and walls on both the floor plan and the elevation drawings.

If there are other things besides a workshop in this location, include those things on the plans. For example, if you have chosen a spot in the garage, include the car, garden tools, bikes, storage cabinets, and so forth. Design for more than one location at this point. Drawing and redrawing plans for alternate locations lets you see all the possibilities and drawbacks of each spot.

At this point it would also be a good idea to make an inventory of all the hand tools and power equipment that you own. Now make a wish list and add it to the original list. Include tools that would make work easier and produce better projects from your workshop.

When you plan your shop, visualize where the workbench, the storage cabinets and drawers, and the stationary power tools will be in relation to one another.

Floor Plan and Elevations

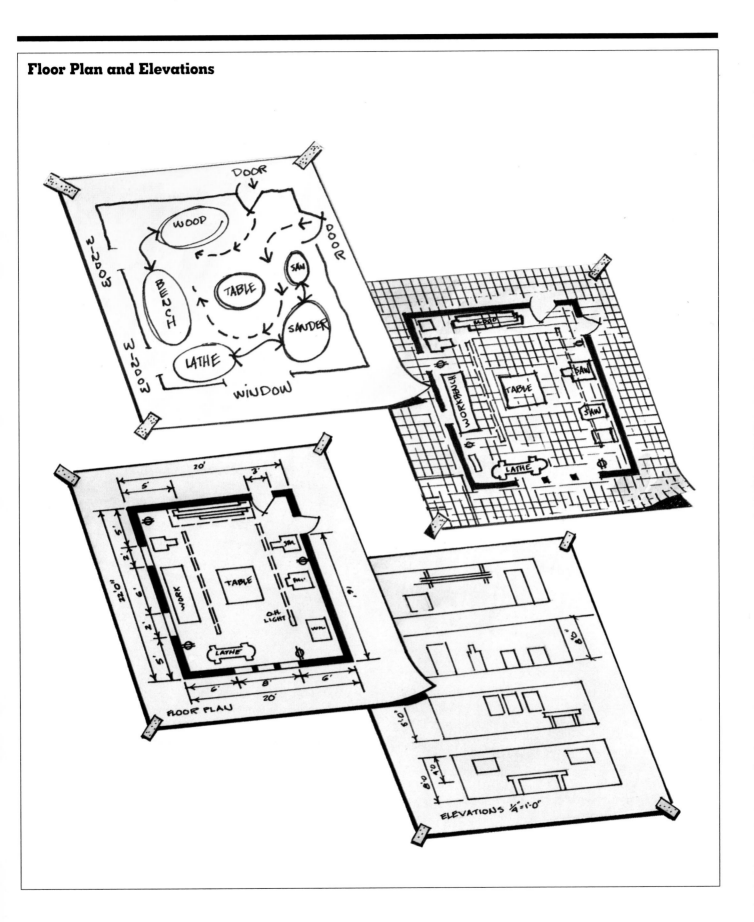

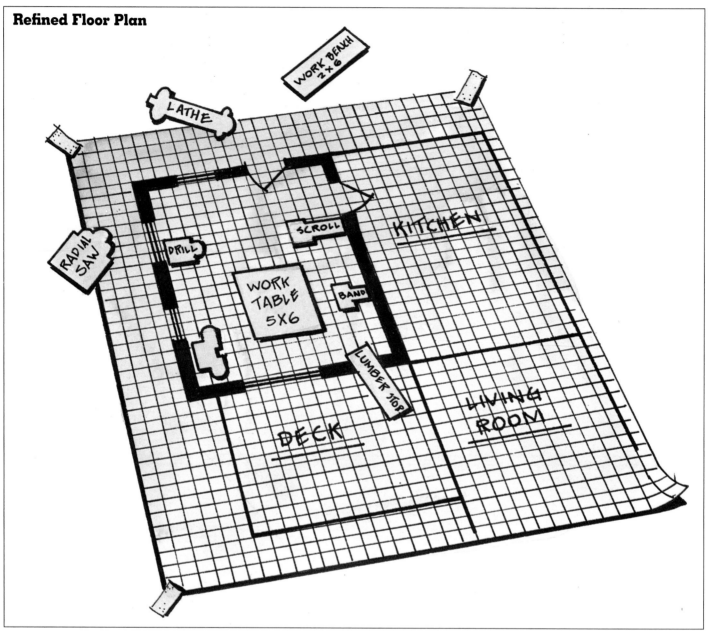

Refine the Floor Plan

Now that you have chosen one or two locations for the shop, it's time to refine the floor plans and the elevation drawings. Letting each ¼-inch square on the graph paper represent 1 foot, draw the perimeter of the new shop. Accurately measure each door and window on the drawing. Include the exact locations and dimensions of outlets, heat vents, pipes and columns, and any other permanent fixtures. This seems tedious, but the time saved in the long run is invaluable.

Place a sheet of tracing paper over the graph paper and on it draw the interior of the new shop. Place the machines with the sequence of operations in mind. For example, in a woodworking shop you will want to move comfortably from sawing to planing to sanding. Place the large pieces of equipment accordingly. Even in a small space, freedom of movement is important. Refine the rough sketch by drawing in your specific requirements. By shifting things around on paper, you can save yourself a lot of work later.

Add an overlay of tracing paper to the elevation drawings and follow the same procedure. Indicate where the shelves will hang, where the bins will fit, and so forth. Be sure not to block windows, doors, or the doors and drawers of closets and cabinets. Take into account the traffic patterns through the shop area. Indicate where heaters, fans, and ventilation will be located.

Tool storage is as individual as each person's work habits. The choice of a tool kit may be determined by something as fundamental as being left- or right-handed. Tool storage may also be determined by the layout of the shop.

A Central Location

All of your tools should be kept in one place. That place should be centrally located, and the tools should be stored in an organized way. Not only will this help you to find each tool quickly, but the edges of planes and other cutting tools stay sharper longer if they are stored correctly.

Tool Kits

Here are some criteria for choosing a tool kit: Can tools be sorted easily? Is it convenient to carry and store? Will it withstand heat, cold, and sudden changes in temperature?

Clear boxes make good containers for tools. Be sure that they are made of strong materials. Humidity and moisture damage tools and hardware, so a toolbox should be as airtight and watertight as possible.

Tool kits should be light enough to be carried to the job site. Each tool should have its own place in the kit, and it should remain there when not in use. Kits may be stored on shelves, under benches, in the tool chest, or in cabinets. Always return the tool kit to its proper place.

Build a Lumber Bin

This unit helps you to organize all kinds of wood materials—plywood sheets, lumber, and molding. Simply a variation on the standard storage bin, it can be designed to meet your own specific needs.

Start by deciding how big the unit will be and how many compartments it will have. Sketch out the various pieces and note the exact dimensions.

Cut all the pieces to size, using ½-inch or ¾-inch plywood for the sides and partition pieces, ¼-inch to ½-inch plywood or hardboard for the back, and ½-inch plywood for the bottom. Use glue and 6-penny (6d) nails or wallboard screws to put the unit together. Assemble the right and left sections separately, gluing and nailing the sides to the partitions. Nail the bottom to both assembled side sections. Then attach the back. Nail on the front pieces last, since they overlap the sides and the bottom.

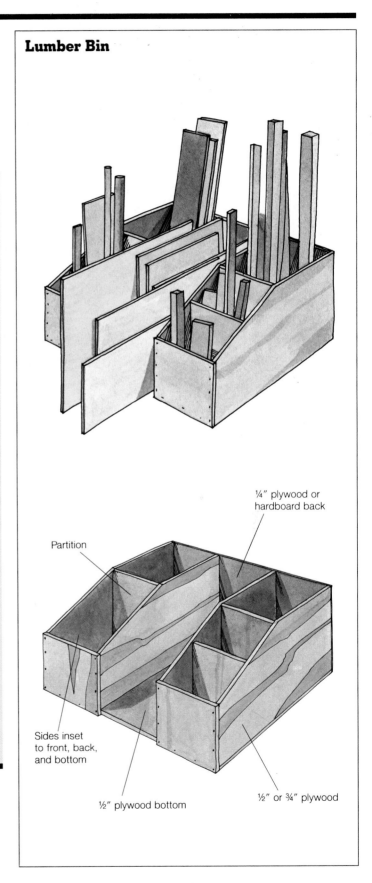

Lumber Bin

¼" plywood or hardboard back

Partition

Sides inset to front, back, and bottom

½" plywood bottom

½" or ¾" plywood

Tool Kits

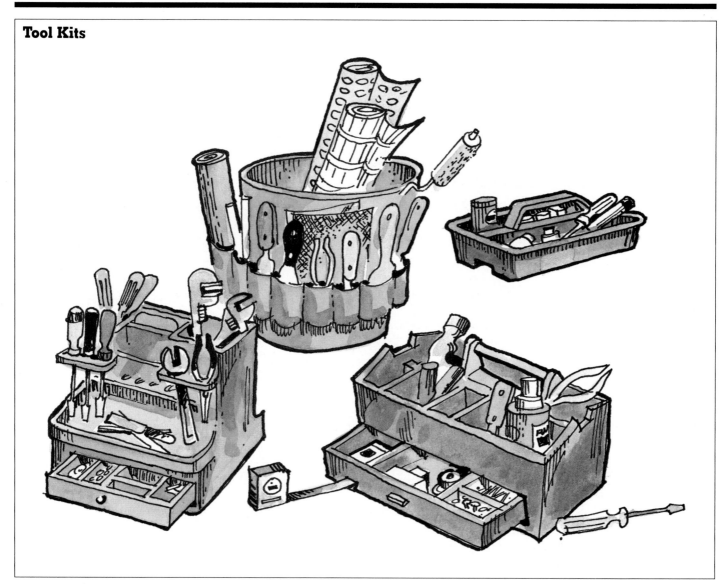

Organizing Kits for Specific Uses

What tools to buy and how to store them depends on what projects you intend to build. Most handicrafters will eventually own an extensive collection of tools dedicated to their particular hobby. However, it would be wise to assemble small kits to handle various jobs around the house. These might include kits for general carpentry, painting and wallboard, plumbing, and electrical work.

Color Coding

If you have several tool kits, color code each one to retain the integrity of each. It is a good idea not to share smaller hand tools among kits. This means that you will probably own several hammers—one each in the tool kits for general carpentry, electrical work, and plumbing—with each color coded to correspond to the kit in which it belongs. The convenience of not having to return to the shop for missing tools is worth the extra price of a few duplicates. Larger and more expensive hand-held power tools will probably have their own place in the shop. They go into the kit when you have a specific job to perform.

Tool Chests and Cabinets

A chest is a fine place to store your best tools. Tools that rattle around in any old box or drawer become nicked and dented; this decreases their quality, renders them less accurate, and makes them harder to work with.

A wall-mounted cabinet provides convenient storage for tools. Hang it just above or near

Tool Cabinet

Workbench Storage Ideas

A single or twin turntable with jars or cans is useful for storing hardware. Need a particular brad? Spin the set to find the appropriate one. These turntables pack a lot of accessible storage into a small space—ideally a corner. Some companies sell rotating holders that can be nailed to the wall or ceiling.

A carousel that is designed for kitchen or office gadgets can be transformed into a stand for paintbrushes and rollers, wallboard supplies, or a collection of screwdrivers and wrenches.

Tool kits stocked and ready to go are indispensable to any workshop. They can be kept at the workbench for everyday use. When necessary, they can be carried to the job site.

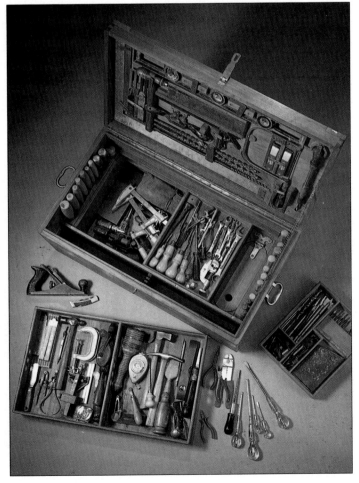

Here is a good example of well-organized tool storage. This portable chest holds a great many tools, thanks to the economical use of interior space.

13

the workbench. When planning any cabinet, first lay out the tools that you will be storing in it. Now check the dimensions of the shelves to make sure that they meet your needs. The doors of the ideal cabinet should have holders for chisels, squares, screwdrivers, and hammers. There should be drawers to hold additional small items. Remember that this is the ideal; your own cabinet need not be this elaborate. It all depends on how many tools you have.

A freestanding cabinet can also be used to store tools. It may contain shelves, drawers, or racks. The cabinet opens to display its contents at a comfortable height and within easy reach. Ideally, the workbench would be only a few steps away. Dovetail joints make the case strong as well as attractive. Cabinet doors, hung on sturdy piano hinges, will not be drooping in a few months under their load of tools.

Tools can be organized in a large filing cabinet containing shallow drawers. These drawers act as metal carrying cases—one for a set of pliers, one for a staple gun and staples, one for a set of Phillips screwdrivers, one for a straight set, and so forth. Using a tape-marking device, label the drawers to show their contents. Attach a paper chart to the outside of the cabinet listing what is in each drawer. This way, if a drawer is taken out, you will know which tools are missing.

Hanging wall cabinets and underbench drawers provide easy access to tools and hardware.

The space under the workbench is put to good use storing supplies and materials. The containers on wheels can be moved anywhere in the shop.

THE HEART OF THE SHOP

You will spend more time at the workbench than anywhere else in the shop. Here you will do handwork, assembly, finishing, and repairs. When you choose a bench, consider the hours you will spend standing, leaning, looking, and moving in this spot. The workbench is indeed the heart of the shop.

Workbench Location

The workbench should be comfortable and highly functional. Don't rush right out to buy one or get the plans to build one until you have considered its location and your needs.

Some people put the workbench in the middle of the shop. Not only can they work on all four sides of the bench, but they are steps away from all of their other equipment. This arrangement saves steps, and it leaves plenty of space for maneuvering large workpieces about.

Other people place the workbench against a wall or on the two sides of a corner. This arrangement leaves less room to maneuver large pieces, but it offers plenty of accessible wall space for storing tools. It can also take advantage of natural light if the bench is placed under or near a window.

The Well-Designed Workbench

The principal criterion for any workbench is sturdiness. Good work requires a solid, horizontal surface, as anyone who has struggled with a flimsy card table will tell you. The bench top should be hip height, so that you can work without stopping. As a rule, this means 30 to 36 inches high. If the bench is to be used for small handicrafts or electrical work, consider one 28 inches high with a stool, for much of this type of work is done sitting down.

Tools should be stored within easy reach. With wall-mounted benches you can hang many tools on the wall itself. Workbenches that stand in the middle of the shop are often constructed with a well to keep tools from rolling off. Both types of benches may be fitted below with cabinets or shelves for increased storage and greater stability.

Purchasing a Workbench

Workbenches can be purchased fully assembled or in kit form. These offer a convenient way to start a new shop. Choose one that either has adjustable legs or is made for your individual working height. Buy the sturdiest bench you can afford.

Height

The first function of the bench is to place work at a convenient height. The height of the bench should be adjusted for your individual comfort and left that way, for unlike a kitchen table, which is used by many people, the workbench is used by only one person. Stand straight and rest the palms of your hands on a surface just high enough so that your elbows are slightly bent. This is your proper upper work height, and the bench should measure this distance from the floor. Working at a bench slightly lower than this can cause back strain after only a few minutes. This height will vary considerably from person to person and may easily surpass the standard 36-inch bench height for tall people.

Low Benches

Although this height is easy on the back and is ideal for most layout, machining, and finishing

If you place the workbench against a wall, you can hang some tools within easy reach.

Workbenches

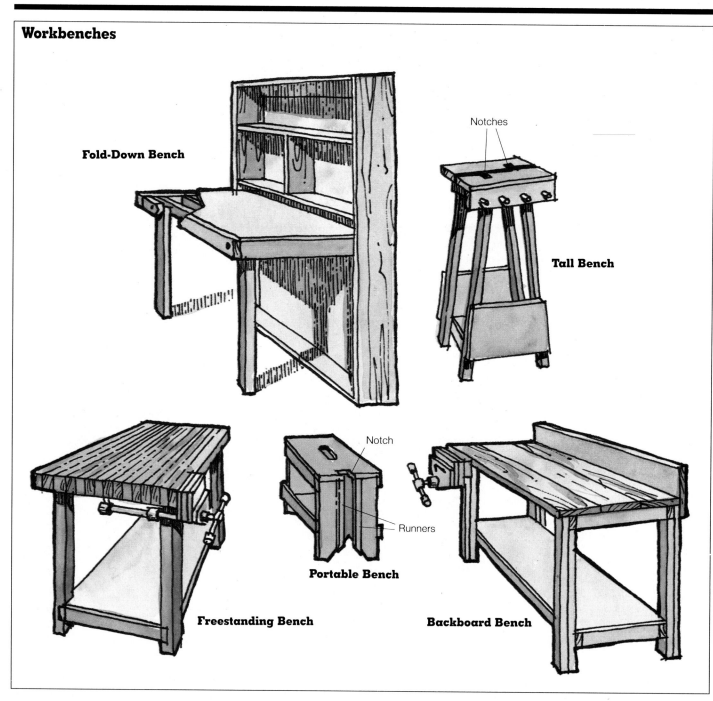

Fold-Down Bench

Tall Bench

Notches

Freestanding Bench

Portable Bench

Notch

Runners

Backboard Bench

operations, it will be too high when you must be on top of your work—when you do hand-sawing, or drill holes with a brace and bit, for example. Years ago carpenters would set up a portable workbench at the job site. It usually consisted of two sturdy sawhorses and several planks, or as often as not an old door stripped of hardware. These low benches were ideal surfaces to hand-saw lumber on and to lay out tools on for the job. Even today such a bench can be set up in minutes with a sturdy piece of plywood and two sawhorses.

Another way to keep a low workstation handy is to install a wood vise low on the corner of the bench so that project parts may be clamped at the correct height for the job.

Make the work surface extra sturdy. Install a braced, heavy bench top consisting of two layers of ¾-inch plywood or laminated 2 by 4 studding. If this is not possible, brace wherever you can to keep the work surface stable. It's difficult to do good work if the table jiggles.

This home-built workbench is mounted on wheels so that it can be moved around within the limited confines of this garage workshop.

Building Your Own Workbench

Building your own workbench is an excellent project. The simple, sturdy design that follows is constructed with basic tools and joints at a fraction of the cost of commercial models. This workbench uses standard building materials with little waste. Make the bench 24 inches wide and choose a length of 4, 6, or 8 feet.

1. Start by ripping a sheet of ¾-inch plywood lengthwise into two pieces. Make sure that one piece is 24 inches wide. The other piece will be slightly narrower, because the saw kerf will be on that side. This does not matter, because the second piece of plywood is for the shelf under the bench, which is narrower than the top.

2. If you are making a 4- or a 6-foot bench, cut the top to length. An 8-foot bench will take the whole piece. Now cut a frame of 2 by 4s to fit under the top. The sides of the frame should be flush with the top edges so that sturdy vises may be bolted to the bench later. Put the frame together with 2½-inch wallboard screws. Then attach the top to the frame with 1⅝-inch wood screws.

3. Using the narrower piece of plywood, cut the shelf to size. The shelf will fit inside the legs. It will be the same length as the top and about 18½ inches wide. Before you cut, double-check the width by laying front and back legs made from 2 by 4s inside the frame of the top and measuring the space between them. This width will vary slightly if the 2 by 4s are not exactly 1⅜ inches wide.

4. Cut the legs to length. Remember to make the workbench a comfortable height for you. Cut the legs ¾ inch short of your ideal working height, because the plywood will fit on top of them. Cut four legs for either a 4-foot or 6-foot bench and six legs for an 8-foot bench. The long bench will sag without the center support.

5. Assemble the bench as follows. Place the top frame upside down. Screw each leg onto the top, one at a time. As you do this check that the leg is square with the top in both directions from the corner. Attach the shelf assembly, using only one screw through each leg. Turn the bench over and double-check the shelf. Is it level? Is it at a convenient height to store items underneath? Once you are satisfied with the position of the shelf, screw it into place as you did the top.

Basic Workbench

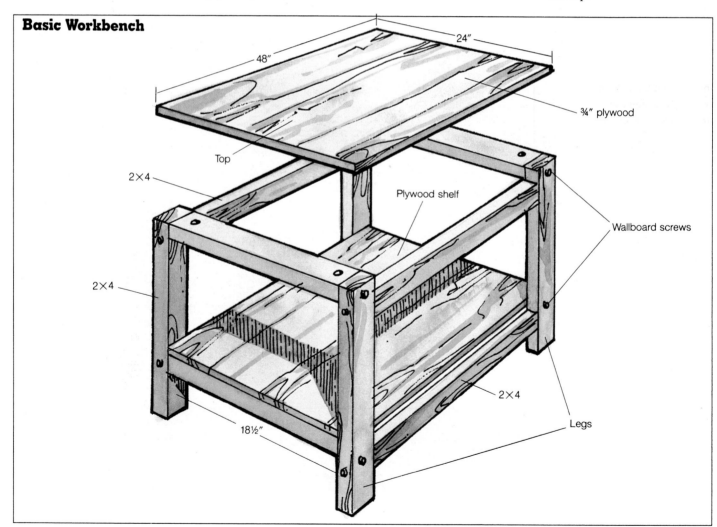

24"

48"

¾" plywood

Top

2×4

Plywood shelf

Wallboard screws

2×4

2×4

18½"

Legs

Building a Fold-Up Bench

This tidy little workbench is designed to fold up and lock when not in use. Folded up it protrudes no more that 14 inches from the wall. Unlocked and folded down it provides two shelves and an open storage bin plus a handy 2 feet by 4 feet of work surface. The unit is made in three parts. First, the back frame and pegboard are installed on the wall. Second, the case and shelves are screwed together, installed over the pegboard frame, and screwed or nailed into place. Finally, the front-and-legs assembly is made and hinged to the case.

1. Start by constructing a flat frame of 1 by 2 lumber. The frame should be 46½ inches long by 22½ inches wide. Cut a sheet of pegboard to the same size and nail it over the frame. Locate studs in the wall and fasten the frame-and-pegboard assembly to the studs with wallboard screws. The bottom of the frame should be ¾ inch higher than your ideal working height. When the bench top is hinged into place, it will fall open at that height. Be sure to level the bottom of the frame when you attach it to the wall.

2. Make the case from 1 by 10 lumber. Crosscut the parts to size. Drill holes in one side piece and in the divider to hold the shelf pegs. (You may want to drill extra holes for an additional shelf.) Be sure that the holes line up vertically and horizontally so that the shelf will sit level. Now nail or screw the box together. Be sure to install the divider far enough forward in the case to make space for the pegboard.

3. Slide the case over the pegboard. It should just fit. Secure it by driving nails or screws through the outside of the case into the pegboard assembly.

4. Now cut the parts for the workbench front and assemble it, using wallboard screws. Install the fold-down legs and leg braces. Finally, secure the front to the case with butt hinges. When the case is open, the workbench will fold down to a level position. There is room for a vise to be mounted on the front edge of the bench top. The front is secured with a hasp at the top in the closed position and may be locked when not in use.

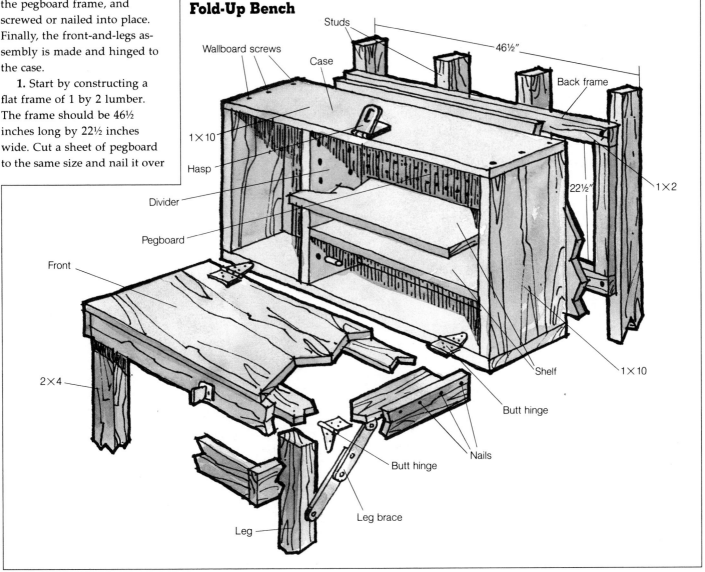

Fold-Up Bench

Studs · Wallboard screws · Case · 46½" · Back frame · 1×10 · Hasp · Divider · 22½" · 1×2 · Pegboard · Front · Shelf · 1×10 · 2×4 · Butt hinge · Nails · Butt hinge · Leg brace · Leg

Make Your Own Sanding Bench

Power Tools Create More Dust

Earlier woodworkers surfaced stock with hand planes and fashioned moldings with specialty planes and scrapers. Cutting was done largely by hand, and smoothing was accomplished with broken glass, planes, and scrapers. Today's woodworkers surface wood with motor-driven planers and jointers, cut with high-speed saws and routers, and smooth with sanders whirring at 12,000 revolutions per minute (rpm).

Hand methods are slower, but they're also quieter and cleaner. The waste chips are large and contribute little to airborne dust. Power woodworking is faster, but it's noisier and dustier. High-speed cutting edges make smaller particles, and these are flung into the air by the circular motion of the machine and by the action of the fan on the motor. Without dust control or respiratory protection, you're breathing directly from that cloud of particles.

Sanding Bench

You can take steps to lower the hazard. When skill and time permit, choose hand tools instead of power tools. Many woodworkers rediscover the high quality and efficiency of hand tools after using power equipment for a few years. However, most people like and need power tools and don't plan to give them up entirely. That is why every shop should have a dust removal system.

The sanding workbench illustrated is one such system. It's easy to install, and although it won't suck up every particle the sander spits out, it will reduce the amount of wood dust in the air. You can easily modify the design to fit your particular needs or adapt it to an existing bench as was done here.

The sanding bench works best when connected to an in-shop dust collection system with a capacity of at least 450 cubic feet per minute. Shop vacuums are less desirable, because they generate relatively low volumes of air and their brush motors are noisy and short-lived. The induction motors of the larger units generate high volume, last a long time, and are quieter.

The basic design consists of a bench top with a dust manifold attached to a box frame on its underside. Dusty air from the sanding operation is drawn down through ¼" holes in the table by clean air moving from the room toward the holes.

1. Drill the holes in the bench top. One way to do this is by taping graph paper to the top and drilling right through it. The chart specifies the right number of holes for air pipes of different sizes. Often the stock being sanded will generate enough dust to start blocking many of the holes. You can compensate by drilling about 50 percent more holes than the chart suggests. When sanding small projects simply cover some of the holes with a sheet of paper.

2. Make the box carefully and caulk the seams to keep it as airtight as possible. Cut a hole in the bottom panel to receive the adapter, which will connect the box to the dust pipe. A recycled rectangular-to-round hot-air vent can be used. Since you may need to clean inside the box from time to time, hinge the top at the back or make it completely removable, held by strips screwed to the bench frame.

3. Any number of custom adaptations are possible. A stop block will hold stock on the table when you are belt sanding. Drill a hole in the two end legs and insert a sturdy dowel to hold rolls of sandpaper. Add a shelf or cabinet below to store tools and other equipment.

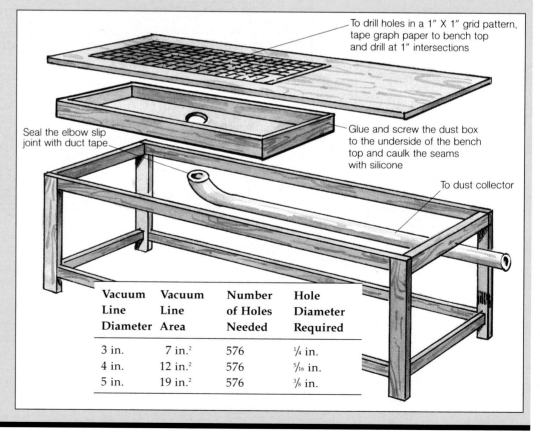

To drill holes in a 1" X 1" grid pattern, tape graph paper to bench top and drill at 1" intersections

Seal the elbow slip joint with duct tape

Glue and screw the dust box to the underside of the bench top and caulk the seams with silicone

To dust collector

Vacuum Line Diameter	Vacuum Line Area	Number of Holes Needed	Hole Diameter Required
3 in.	7 in.²	576	¼ in.
4 in.	12 in.²	576	5/16 in.
5 in.	19 in.²	576	3/8 in.

Portable Tool Totes

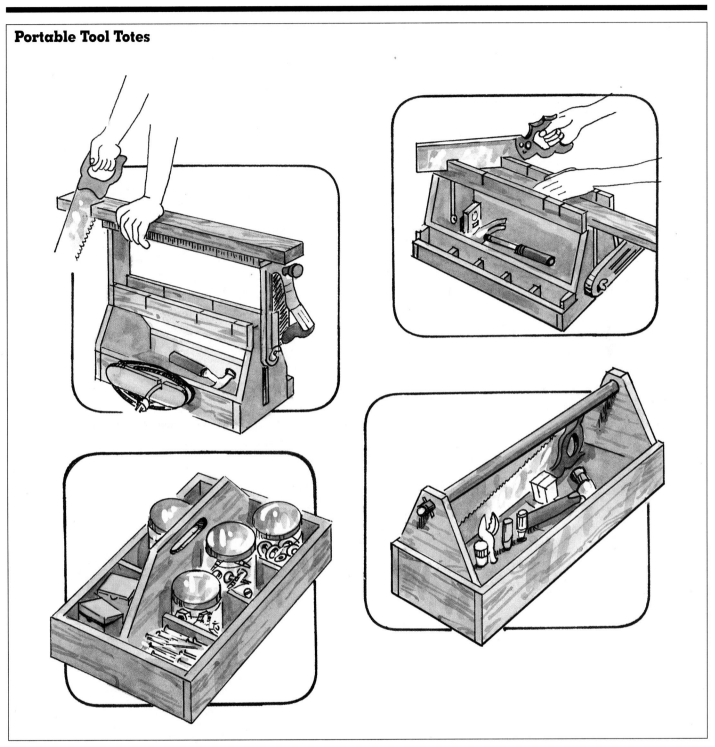

Portability

When you work on stationary fixtures such as showers and sinks, individual portable tool kits are essential.

Add a mobile workbench and you're in business. A power unit built into the bench and a few high-quality extension cords bring you to the job site ready to get going.

Tool Aprons and Tool Belts

Carpenter's aprons and tool belts can make even the novice feel like a professional.

Each tool has its own place on the belt or apron, which serves as a mobile kit. Between jobs you can hang it in the closet.

Workbench Vises

Equip the bench with a sturdy vise to hold your work in place. The handiest, all-around model is a bench vise with a swivel base, pipe jaws below the main jaws, and a small anvil in the rear. It can be used to secure parts for matching, as a small anvil to form parts, or to hold pipes for threading and cutting; and it can be fitted with soft jaws to hold wood without marring the surface.

A good woodworking vise is mounted on the side of the workbench flush with the bench top. The metal jaws of the vise are flat to protect the surface of the workpiece, but handicrafters usually attach replaceable wood blocks to both jaws for further protection. Slide-up bars, which are called dogs and are located in the outward jaw, secure long pieces of stock against other dogs inserted in the bench top. There is a series of square holes on the bench top designed to fit various lengths of stock. A dog is inserted at the appropriate spot in the bench, and the dog in the vise is raised to clamp the stock flat on the bench top as the vise is closed. This clamping system lies flush with the top surface of the bench. It permits long planing strokes or sanding operations.

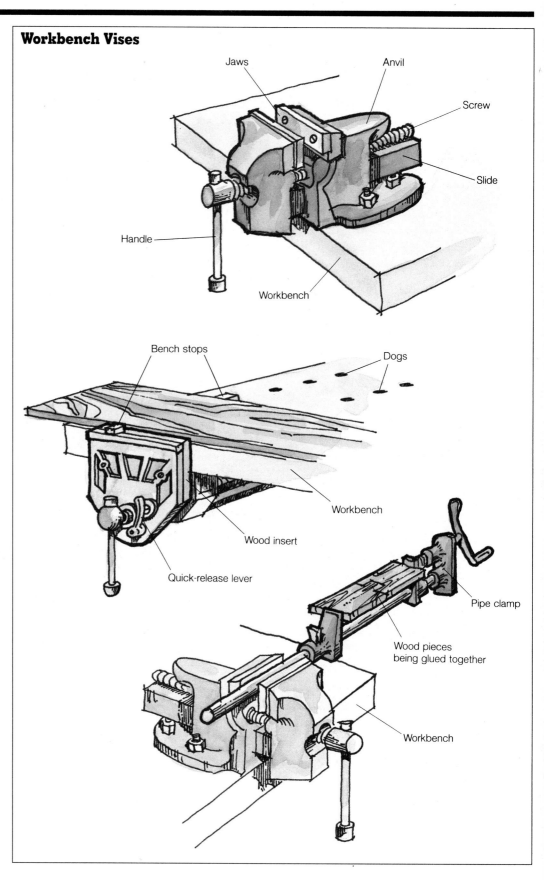

Workbench Vises

Jaws · Anvil · Screw · Slide · Handle · Workbench

Bench stops · Dogs · Workbench · Wood insert · Quick-release lever

Pipe clamp · Wood pieces being glued together · Workbench

Clamps

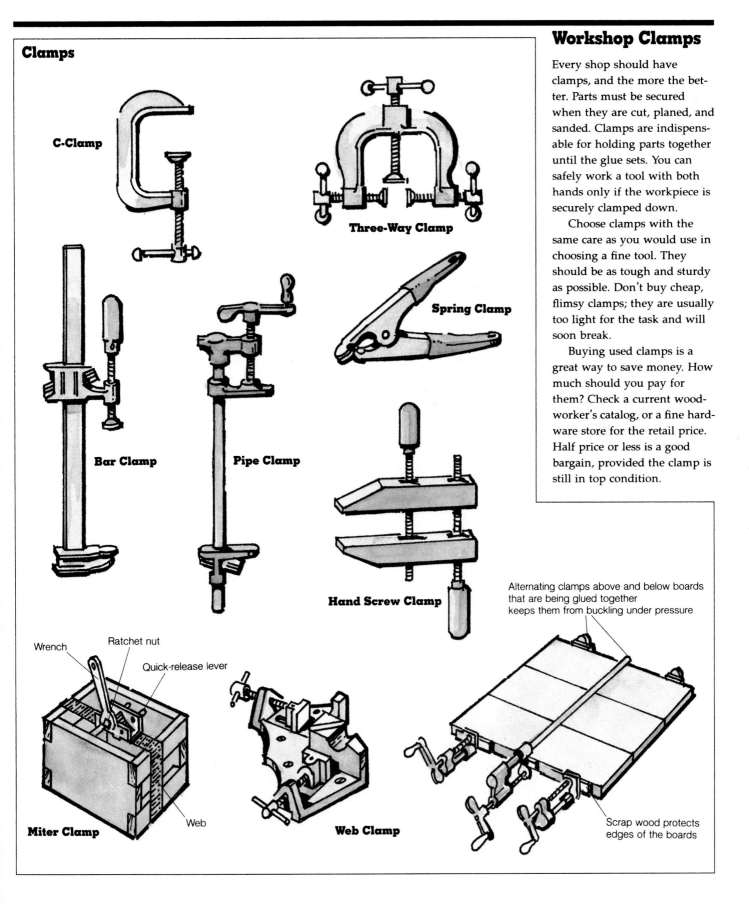

C-Clamp

Three-Way Clamp

Spring Clamp

Bar Clamp

Pipe Clamp

Hand Screw Clamp

Wrench

Ratchet nut

Quick-release lever

Web

Miter Clamp

Web Clamp

Alternating clamps above and below boards that are being glued together keeps them from buckling under pressure

Scrap wood protects edges of the boards

Workshop Clamps

Every shop should have clamps, and the more the better. Parts must be secured when they are cut, planed, and sanded. Clamps are indispensable for holding parts together until the glue sets. You can safely work a tool with both hands only if the workpiece is securely clamped down.

Choose clamps with the same care as you would use in choosing a fine tool. They should be as tough and sturdy as possible. Don't buy cheap, flimsy clamps; they are usually too light for the task and will soon break.

Buying used clamps is a great way to save money. How much should you pay for them? Check a current woodworker's catalog, or a fine hardware store for the retail price. Half price or less is a good bargain, provided the clamp is still in top condition.

THE ELEMENTS OF A WORKSHOP

The important elements of a fine home workshop are discussed in this section in detail. Ideas for accomplishing goals and overcoming problems are presented. They apply to all types of workshops, so read through this section with your floor plans close at hand.

Room Dimensions

If the shop is to be used primarily for woodworking, the minimum recommended area is 75 square feet; 100 square feet would be better. An ideal shop would measure 125 square feet, and to this would be added a lumber storage area 16 feet long and 7 feet wide. The size of the shop, of course, will determine the number of stationary power tools that it will hold.

For a shop focusing on crafts or electrical work, a minimum of 50 and a maximum of 75 square feet is recommended. This smaller area still allows for adequate storage, since tools and supplies for these projects take up less space. The workbench should be designed for sitting rather than for standing. If the surface is more than 28 or 30 inches high, you will need a stool or adjustable chair.

Access and Movement

When you build large woodworking projects, you will be moving long pieces of lumber around, so consider carefully the space and size requirements of benches and machine tools.

The Workbench

The bench should be located 4 feet from freestanding machines, which in turn should be located about 3 feet apart. If space is so limited that this is not feasible, install rolling bases on these machines. They can be moved into a center space for use and then rolled back into a corner for convenient storage.

Heavy-Duty Power Equipment

Allow 12 to 16 feet front and back to feed stock to a table saw, planer, or jointer. Allow the same amount of side clearance with band saws and radial arm saws to accommodate the swing factor.

Mounting Large Tools Near One Another

A grinder, a vertical band saw, and a drill press can be mounted back-to-back.

Traffic Flow

You should not be standing in a traffic path when you are working. To avoid this problem position the equipment at a slight angle. You will need to

In this spacious barn workshop, there is enough room around the machinery to work on large projects.

Machines in Sequence

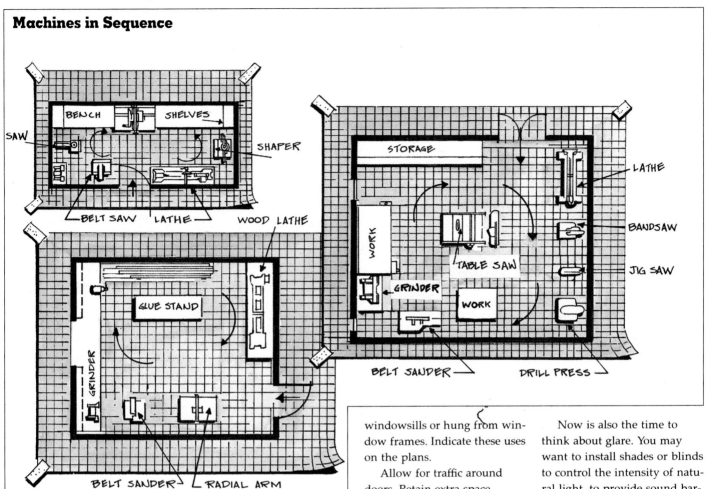

move materials in and out of the shop. Provide doors or windows for doing this and show them on the floor plan.

Machines in Sequence

When you plan the workshop, remember that you will want to move easily from one part of a project to another. Items used in sequence should be kept close together. For example, the circular saw, jointer, and planer belong together and near the lumber. Good planning now can save miles of walking later.

Windows and Doors

Show the swing of doors and windows on the floor plan. The symbol for this is a quarter circle drawn from the hinge side. On both the floor plan and the elevation drawings, show how you might use the fronts and backs of doors for light shelving, pegboards, or other small-tool storage. Small tools can also be kept on windowsills or hung from window frames. Indicate these uses on the plans.

Allow for traffic around doors. Retain extra space around stationary machinery. If a machine is near a door, leave room for bringing in materials and equipment.

Natural Lighting, Electric Lighting, and Color

Proper lighting should be high on your checklist. Handcrafts and other small projects require strong light. Natural sunlight is ideal. Adding windows or skylights or simply removing obstructions from existing windows can bolster the light meter reading for the shop.

Now is also the time to think about glare. You may want to install shades or blinds to control the intensity of natural light, to provide sound barriers, and to give privacy at night. Be sure to position machines and benches so that bright sunlight cannot shine directly into your eyes.

Because you will also be working on rainy days and at night, you will need artificial lighting as well.

Reflected light can be an asset in any workshop. Paint the ceilings and walls white or off-white. Furniture and other equipment should be painted in colors comfortable to the eye. Bright red, yellow, and black should be reserved for safety markers.

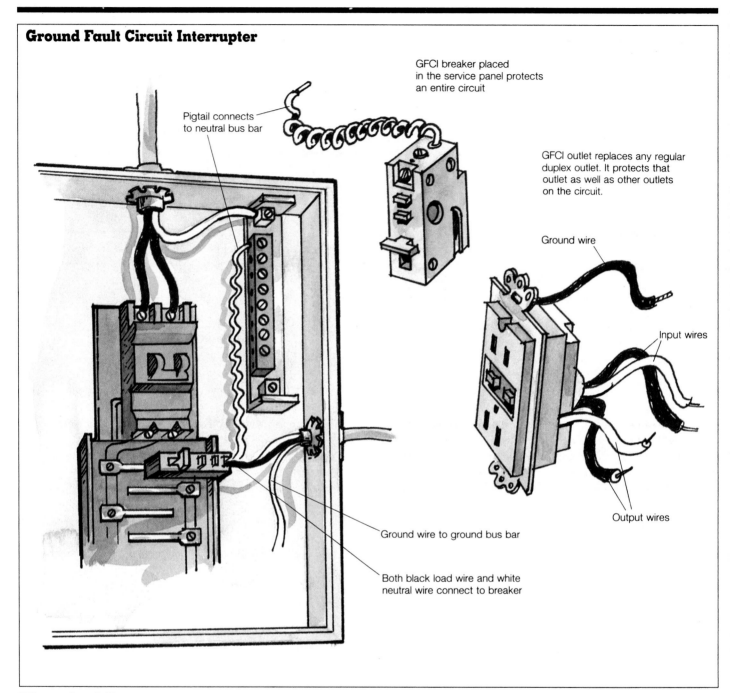

Ground Fault Circuit Interrupter

Pigtail connects to neutral bus bar

GFCI breaker placed in the service panel protects an entire circuit

GFCI outlet replaces any regular duplex outlet. It protects that outlet as well as other outlets on the circuit.

Ground wire

Input wires

Output wires

Ground wire to ground bus bar

Both black load wire and white neutral wire connect to breaker

Electrical Power

Residential areas are provided with single-phase 120- and 240-volt service. Industrial areas are provided with three-phase power. You will probably need 120-volt circuits for most of the machines and a few 240-volt circuits for heavier stationary machines, such as an arc welder or a surface planer. If a machine is rated to run at either 110 or 220 volts, it is best to wire it at the higher voltage. All of the circuits except for the lighting circuit should be provided with locks. This will allow the shop to be lit while the rest of the power is off—a vital safeguard when small children are about, or when you are not in the shop.

It isn't difficult to determine the power requirements of the shop. Each machine, whether hand-held or stationary, is rated at the number of ampere hours it uses under load. Most hand-held power tools use less than 10 amperes. Stationary tools use more. Do not rely on horsepower ratings for these calculations. Manufacturers use different systems to rate horsepower. Go by the number of amperes the tool uses.

First, determine the maximum number of tools and appliances that are likely to be in use at any one time. For example, the radial arm saw may be in use with a vacuum attachment at the same time as the overhead fan and the lights are on. Perhaps the fan in the spray booth is on as well. Add up the total number of ampere hours from each motor rating; then add the lights. This is the absolute minimum number of amperes required to run the shop. Design the electrical system to carry at least double this load, particularly if two people may be using power in the shop at the same time.

You will notice that the ampere ratings on 240-volt motors are usually lower than the ratings on 120-volt motors of the same size. That is because 240-volt applications are supplied with two 120-volt lines that, when added together, supply 240 volts. The two lines come from separate legs, or bars, of the subpanel. The motor will have four wires—one neutral (white), one ground (green or bare), and the two 120-volt power lines (usually black and red). With two 120-volt lines supplying power to the motor, the wire size may remain standard and the wire stay cooler under the flow of electricity. When calculating the total number of amperes the motor requires, double the ratings under one leg. For instance, the

motor may be labeled at 9 amperes per leg. The total power requirements will be 18 amperes.

Determine the number of powered circuits that you will need to supply the shop. This is influenced by the location of the tools that draw the most power. It is wise to have a qualified electrician plan and install the circuits. Plan the layout in such a way that the load on each circuit will not exceed the maximum rating of that circuit. Otherwise the breaker will keep shutting off the power.

Most hand-held tools require 5 to 20 amperes of power at 120 volts. Some stationary woodworking equipment requires 220 volts.

You may not need to add new outlets. Consider enhancing access to the present ones by installing a power strip. This will not provide more electricity, but it will give you more plugs at convenient locations. The total available electricity is controlled by the carrying capacity of the circuit into which the power strip is plugged. If the circuit is rated at 15 amperes of power at 120 volts, it will carry a total of 1,800 watts. You may not exceed this total or the fuse will blow. It is easy blow a fuse or

trip a circuit breaker if you plug too many tools into the power strip and turn them all on at once. If you need more electrical power than the circuit is designed for, install another circuit.

Ground fault circuit interrupters (GFCIs) should be installed in a kitchen or basement workshop. These safety devices sense the slightest short. They may be an integral part of the circuit breaker, or they may be installed in the first outlet of each circuit. If they are wired into an outlet, they will protect that outlet and any other outlet that receives power from it. Mark the locations of all outlets, lights, and boxes on the floor plan and elevation drawings. If you are unfamiliar with electrical wiring techniques you should have a licensed electrician advise you or actually perform the work.

If extension cords are on your list of supplies, make sure that they are approved for the amount of current that they will carry. Heavy-duty grounded cords with three-prong plugs will meet most needs. The cords should be made from No. 16 or heavier wire. Remember the rule about quality—the cheap version could be just that! Inexpensive extension cords are apt to be made of light wire that heats up under load.

A reel-in extension cord comes in handy in any shop. Hung from the ceiling it will be out of the way when not in use.

Heating, Cooling, and Humidity Control

The workshop should be comfortable all year around. If it is in a shed or other unheated structure, you will want to heat it for your own comfort and to provide the proper environment for materials and tools. Wood and many other handicraft materials are affected by fluctuations in humidity and temperature. If the shop is allowed to cool past the dew point, condensation will rust metal tools. Extreme heat and cold can also affect the performance of power tools.

Paint should be stored at moderate temperatures. Finishing materials are applied at room temperature for best results. Water-based paints are ruined when they freeze.

Noise

If shop noises will disturb other people, you may need soundproofing. Excessive noise is dangerous for you, too. Noise can disrupt your concentration. It can fatigue you to the danger point, increasing your chance of injuring yourself. Loud noise over a prolonged period can even damage your hearing. Fortunately there are many ways to reduce noise within your shop and from the shop to the outside.

Ear Protection

Always protect your ears. Wear ear guards and insist that anyone who uses the shop also wear them.

Sound Deadeners

Fire-retardant wall rugs or acoustic tiles deaden sound and are easy to install. These materials trap air in small pockets that transmit sound poorly. Walls can also be constructed with double studding and insulation to deaden the transmission of sound.

Constructing a raised wood floor on top of a concrete floor can help to reduce noise. Acoustic ceiling tile can be installed between or underneath the floor joists to absorb sound.

If there are pipes or columns in a basement workshop, don't place machines near them. They will transmit the noise and vibrations with unbelievable success. Your furnace might as well be a set of stereo speakers if you set up a table saw near the duct work. Use those spaces for handwork or storage. Save another corner for the buzzing saws.

If you live in an apartment or a condominium, discuss your plans with the neighbors. You will need to know the floor plans of their apartments. Don't set up that saw next to someone's bedroom wall.

Ventilation and Dust Control

When you work with tools, it's important to stay alert and refreshed, so you will need a ventilation system in the shop.

Include it on the floor plan and the elevation drawings. Dust and fumes must be carried out as fresh air is carried in.

One easy answer is to install an exhaust fan. To install one you may have to remove part of one window or a small section of wall. The fan should be placed right behind the finishing area of the shop and located so that fumes from solvents, glues, or paints move away from you toward the outside. Never work between the exhaust fan and your project, because you will be exposed to harmful fumes. Place the exhaust fan where fumes that are forced outside do not find their way back inside through windows, doors, or fresh-air intakes. The exhaust fan outlet should be placed where prevailing winds or the flow of air around the house will quickly disperse these fumes away from buildings. If you are using an existing exhaust, such as the one in the kitchen hood, *be sure that it is venting outside.*

Although sanding dust may be exhausted outside, it is usually piped into a vacuum or dust removal system, filtered, and exhausted back into the shop. This conserves the heated air. It is important to remember that a dust collection system *will not filter out fumes* from paints and solvents. These fumes will go right through the system and flow back inside. Although dust and chips may be filtered, fumes from solvents, paints, and so forth must be exhausted safely outside.

This saw has been equipped with a permanently installed vacuum dust removal system.

Installing a Fan in a Stud Wall

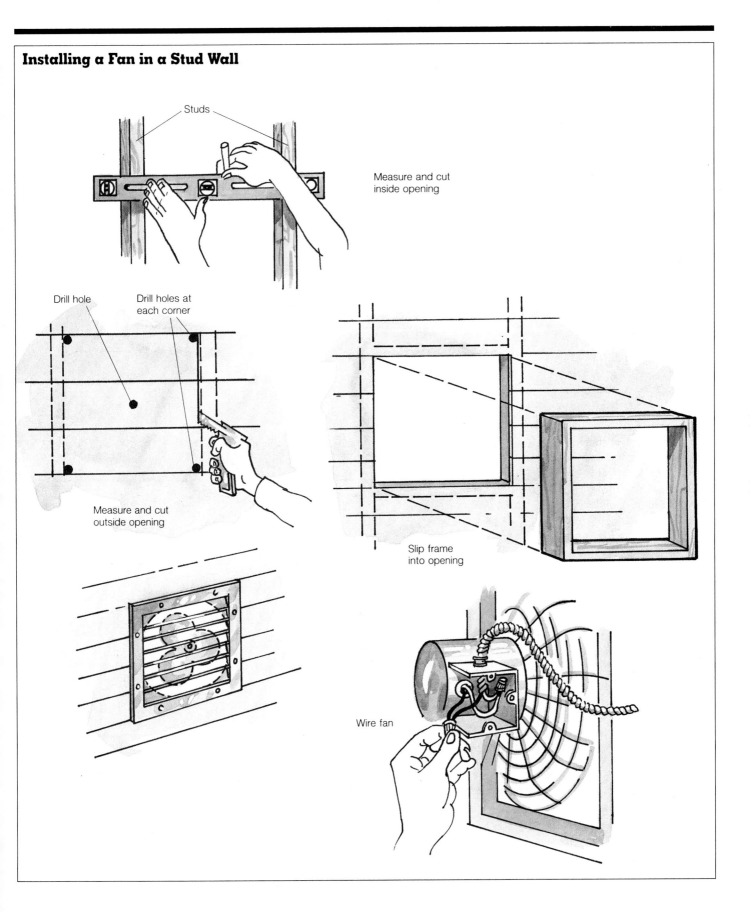

Studs

Measure and cut inside opening

Drill hole

Drill holes at each corner

Measure and cut outside opening

Slip frame into opening

Wire fan

Special Needs

A tall person can be very uncomfortable working at a bench made for a short person, and vice versa. Benches and shelves must meet the user's special needs. When building shelves and benches for the shop, determine the most comfortable height for you and anyone else who will be using them. The top of a standard workbench measures about 36 inches from the floor, but you might find a height of 32 inches or 40 inches more comfortable. The height of shelves and the position of cabinets should also take individual differences into account.

Every shop should have at least one stool, since standing for long periods is tiring. Two stools or benches make it possible to work with a friend or spouse. Stools or chairs on casters are preferable to stationary chairs, because they are easily moved around.

If the shop is in a basement with low pipes or beams, you may want to mark them with reflective or colored tape to warn tall people to duck.

Visual Handicaps

People with limited vision usually require bright lighting. Additional lights along with brightly colored paint or tape can help them to locate and identify tools, bench edges, and equipment storage areas. If there are stairs, painted tread nosings are a must. For close work consider a magnifier light that can be clamped to the bench. Safety goggles with magnifying lenses protect the eyes while they improve vision. Magnifying sheets enlarge the print on small diagrams.

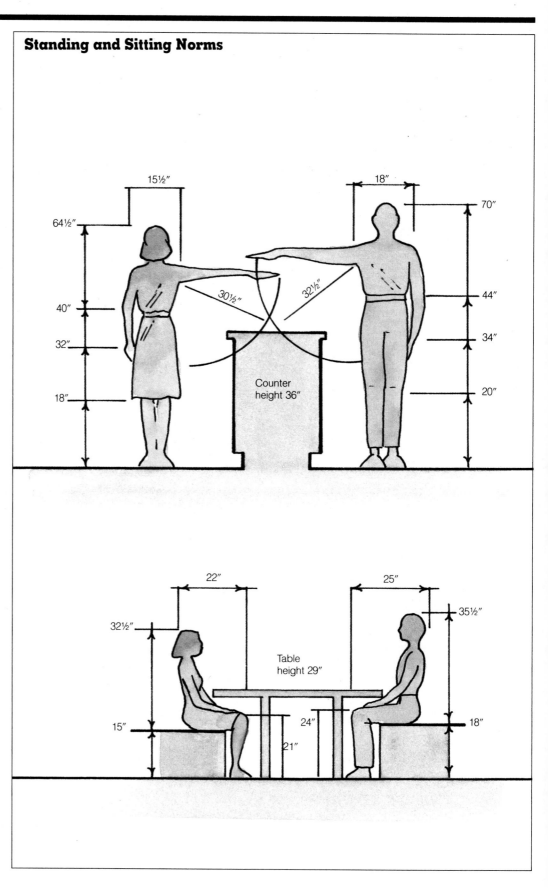

Standing and Sitting Norms

Adjustment for a Wheelchair

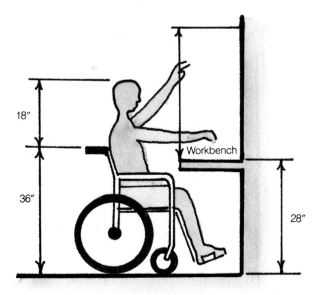

18"

36"

Workbench

28"

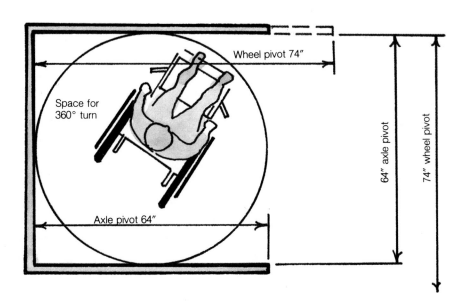

Wheel pivot 74"

Space for 360° turn

64" axle pivot

74" wheel pivot

Axle pivot 64"

Wheelchairs

Using a wheelchair in a shop means adjusting the height of the workbench. A 28-inch or 30-inch bench should be about right. The front legs of wall-mounted benches may be removed to provide wheelchair access. The top should be supported with diagonal bracing to the base of the back wall.

A special board that fits across the arms of the wheelchair can be made for closeup jobs (soldering electrical circuitry or jewelry, for example). This eliminates leaning to reach over a bench. A tool belt for the chair can include a magnetic pickup device and a set of grabbers. The space between the bench and floor-mounted equipment must be wide enough to accommodate the wheelchair. You should also consider where your eyes will be in relation to this equipment when you plan its location. Be sure that you can move about the shop easily.

Deafness

A flashing light system is available to warn you that a tool is still running. A red light is often hung from the center of the shop to indicate that the master switch is on.

Children

Your children can enjoy working with you in the shop. However, unless they are closely supervised by an adult, a shop is a dangerous place for children. A brightly colored master switch should be located at the entrance, well out of a child's reach. It will shut off power to everything except the lights. Install a kill switch for each

Refuse Collection

Open-ended plywood box, enclosing all but the working face of a radial arm saw, stops sawdust blown toward the back wall and drops it to the bottom, where an opening accommodates the cuff of a vacuum hose connected to a shop vacuum and canister

Enclosed chute built into an opening in the workbench funnels shavings into a movable bin

Fireproof metal container for rags

major power tool as well. The door should have a lock so that there will be no unsupervised visits from small fry.

Waste Removal and Fire Hazards

In the workshop you will have to deal with many hazardous wastes. Know how and where to store them. Call a local sanitation company to find out how to dispose of them. The cooperative extension offices in most counties also have information concerning the use, handling, and disposal of these products. The shop should have metal cabinets with locks for storing paints and other toxic materials. When handling toxics know the antidotes. Post a chart in the shop with first-aid information.

A shop, with its abundance of electrical circuits, motors, and combustibles, must be examined carefully for fire hazards. Be sure that the exits open quickly and easily. You will need a fire extinguisher that works, smoke detectors with lights, and the telephone number of the fire department. For a large shop you might consider installing a sprinkler system. Keep a chart on the wall with instructions for putting out different types of fires. Store oily rags in a fireproof metal container and dispose of them according to the regulations in your community pertaining to toxic waste. Don't allow sawdust to pile up and get damp. This can create spontaneous combustion. Clutter in the corners and along the floor is a fire hazard as well as a nuisance. Not only does a neat, orderly shop provide unobstructed escape routes, but it also contains less fuel.

Evaluate Your Plans

When you are satisfied with the floor plan and the elevation drawings, go to the shop site and double-check the design. Compare the plan with the available space and ask yourself these questions: Will there be enough light? Will I be able to move easily from one piece of equipment to another? Where will the ventilation be? Is there an area for cleaning supplies? Is there a storage area that I have overlooked? This will test the plan and will give you a chance to make changes and additions. After the shop is built, continue to evaluate its workability. Using it, you will learn far more about the strengths and weaknesses of your design. If necessary, you can make further changes later.

Safety Rules

The safety rules for workshops can be stated in one sentence. Treat your tools with understanding and respect. Always understand the function of each tool and know how it should be used before you use it. This applies especially to power tools.

• Read instructions carefully, practice, and proceed slowly.
• Don't be afraid of tools. If correctly used they'll do your bidding.
• Pay close attention to what you're doing. A slip in concentration can result in a damaged board or tool—or hand.
• Keep the shop neat and dry. A messy workshop easily

becomes a series of booby traps. These cause accidents that could have been avoided.
• Always unplug power tools when they are not in use. Always unplug them when you change bits or blades. Always use double-insulated tools, proper wiring, and appropriate extension cords.
• Keep cords out of the path of blades and bits.
• Most high-speed operations, such as cutting with a radial arm saw, produce both chips and noise. Safety glasses and ear guards protect you against these hazards. Wearing them also increases your level of concentration.

Basic Safety Outfit

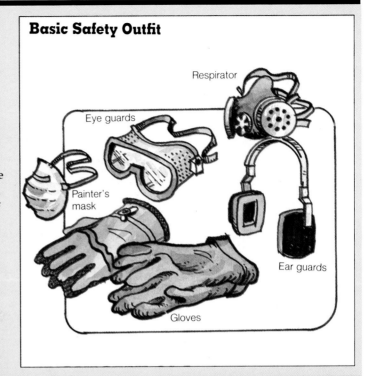

Respirator

Eye guards

Painter's mask

Ear guards

Gloves

Safety in the Shop

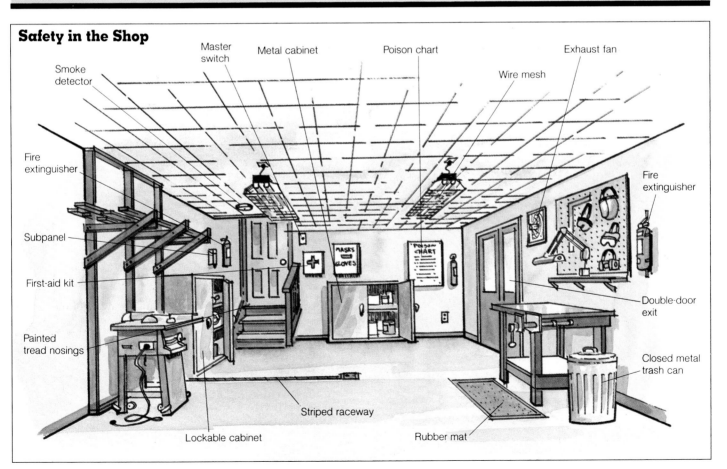

Smoke detector

Master switch

Metal cabinet

Poison chart

Exhaust fan

Wire mesh

Fire extinguisher

Subpanel

First-aid kit

Painted tread nosings

Lockable cabinet

Striped raceway

Rubber mat

Fire extinguisher

Double-door exit

Closed metal trash can

33

STORAGE DETAILS

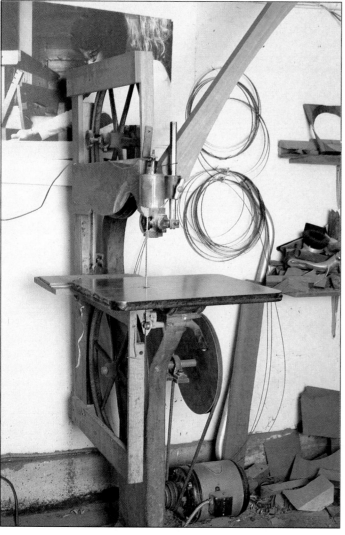

Easy access to tools and hardware sometimes requires innovation.
Opposite, top and bottom left: Here are ways to store drill and router bits and bandsaw blades.
Opposite, top right: The handy file and rasp holder can be placed anywhere.
Opposite, bottom right: Tight quarters demand efficient storage; an old filing cabinet and a toolbox on wheels do the job here.
Top left: A corner doesn't go to waste when supplies and hardware are neatly stored in a wall cabinet and on open shelves.
Bottom: You can tell at a glance what kind of nails and screws are in this cabinet; just look at the samples that are fastened to the outside of each drawer.

SMALL-SPACE WORKSHOPS

Good things can happen in small spaces. Even if you live in a studio apartment, don't discount the possibility of a home workshop. The quarters may be cramped or shared with other household activities, but by using your ingenuity you can probably find several places to set up your shop.

You'll be spending a lot of time in this workshop, so choose a spot that you will enjoy. With some planning even the smallest area can be made to work.

A spare room across from the living room has been converted into a workshop in this small home.

A KITCHEN CORNER

What better place to establish a small workshop than in the kitchen with its many cupboards and drawers? Why not take a corner and transform it?

Kitchen Cabinets

Most kitchen cabinets consist of an upper unit, which contains shelves, and a base unit, which may have shelves or drawers. There is a sturdy counter on the base unit. Dimensions of a base unit are between 23 and 25 inches deep and between 34 and 36 inches high, with a 15- to 20-inch door opening. (Measure your own cabinets, though; they may be custom-made.) Each of these units can become the foundation of a very good workshop.

Organization will be the main job here. Look carefully at all of the available space. There is space under the upper cabinet—perhaps a good place for a mounted light or a cookbook rack to hold plans. The sides, if they are not attached to other units, are fine for brackets and mounting holders. Things that should be kept out of a child's reach can go along the ceiling on top of the upper cabinet. A deep cabinet closet might be just right to store a roll-out tool kit. You might install child-proof catches on the cabinet doors as well.

Workbenches in the Kitchen

You will need a work surface that can be spilled upon, hammered on, and generally beaten up. You can use the kitchen table if necessary, but it should be protected. Have a piece of particleboard or plywood cut to fit over it. A cover board for the whole table might be too heavy to lift, so cover only the part of the table that you will work on. You might store this cover board where the extra table leaves are kept.

Kitchen Corner Workshop

Your workbench could also be a transformed butcher block. Lockable casters enable you to move this bench anywhere you need it.

Organizing Storage in Cupboards and Drawers

Moisture is ever-present in the kitchen, and hardware kept uncovered in a closed drawer will rust. Store it in tightly sealed jars or other containers.

You will need a carrier for tools. Many carriers have handles, and some have wheels. Old tackle boxes and sewing boxes make excellent totes for plumbing supplies, as do clear plastic boxes and stackable bins. You can also build a portable tool kit that rolls out of a cupboard. Alternatively, you can buy and adapt a cleaning tote.

Other adaptations include turning a carousel for cooking utensils into a merry-go-round for screwdrivers, paintbrushes, or wrenches. Plastic-coated webbed shelving can double the tool storage space in a cupboard. Turntables, undershelf drawers, and cup hangers are further options.

A kitchen drawer in or near the work area can be organized into sections with homemade wood dividers or with plastic trays. Into these go masking, duct, and electrician's tapes along with an assortment of wallboard screws, nails, and other small hardware necessities.

Organized Storage

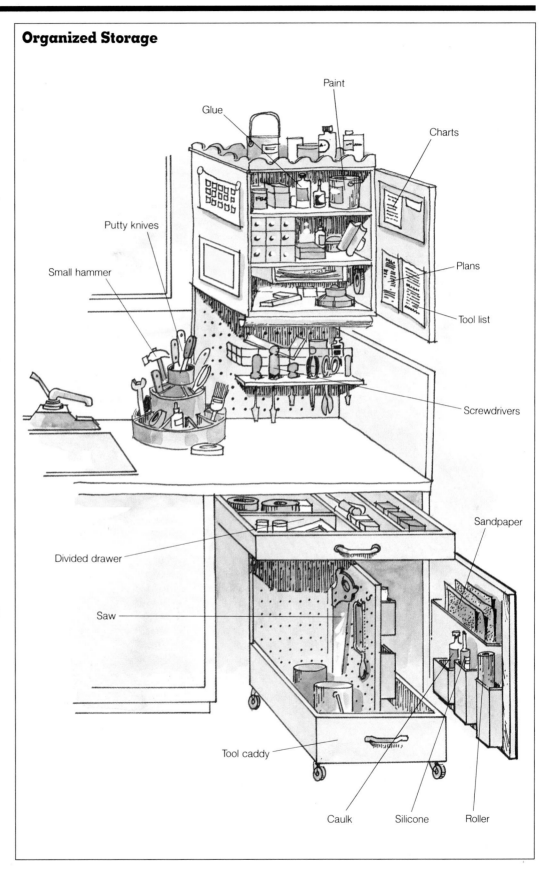

Paint

Glue

Charts

Putty knives

Plans

Small hammer

Tool list

Screwdrivers

Sandpaper

Divided drawer

Saw

Tool caddy

Caulk

Silicone

Roller

How to Build a Kitchen Roll-Out Tote

This tote fits the contours of the bottom of a cupboard, allowing space for movement in and out. It rolls on a simple sliding base or on small casters. On the left side attach a triangular piece of pegboard firmly to the inside of the box, which is just smaller than the inside height of the cupboard. Here you can hang a pair of pliers, a wrench, and a couple of paintbrushes. Make a cutout in the top of this to serve as a handle. The box should have compartments to suit your needs. The one in the illustration is being used for household maintenance, so it includes basic kits for paint, plumbing, wall repair, and carpentry. On the right side of the cupboard itself, mount a magnetic clip for putty knives and scrapers. A broom clamp or two can be added to hold a hammer and a plunger. (If they don't fit here, store them in the broom closet.) These tools should not hang down into the box. Make sure that they clear it, so the unit can roll in and out easily.

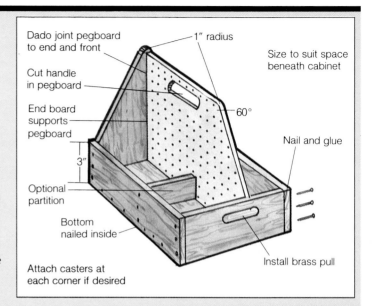

Dado joint pegboard to end and front

1" radius

Size to suit space beneath cabinet

Cut handle in pegboard

End board supports pegboard

60°

Nail and glue

3"

Optional partition

Bottom nailed inside

Install brass pull

Attach casters at each corner if desired

It's easy to see what the priorities are in this home workshop—the workbench serves as a kitchen table, rather than the other way around.

Water

The ready availability of water makes a kitchen workshop great for cleanup. Not many other locations can boast this advantage. Install dispensers of heavy-duty hand cleaner and hand lotion near the sink. Have a fire extinguisher and a box of baking soda nearby too. These safeguards belong in the kitchen anyway.

Lighting

Over-the-counter fluorescent lighting is easily installed. Modern units have a bracket that screws into the molding or the underside of existing cabinets. Illumination should be very strong, especially for detailed work. Plan for an undercabinet fluorescent lamp that gives at least 1,500 footcandles of light.

Electrical Outlets

Most kitchens are wired for large appliances and have three-prong grounded outlets. A power strip with an on-off switch can be mounted above the workbench. If possible, avoid working close to the sink, but if that is the only available work space, use ground fault circuit interrupters (GFCIs). These shut down all power at the slightest short.

Hazardous Materials

Since the kitchen is filled with food, you must be extremely careful with chemicals and fumes. Consider going outside or into another area when you work with hazardous materials. Always cover food, as well as dishes and utensils, when using toxic or potentially toxic substances.

Tools for the Kitchen Corner

Space will determine the size of your tool collection, but some basics are a must. The tools on the following list are adequate to deal with almost any repair emergency or woodworking project.

Woodwork and Electric
- Label maker
- Clipboard
- Fire extinguisher
- Electrician's screwdriver
- Nos. 0, 1, 2, lead pencils
- Phillips screwdriver
- Fine-blade ruler
- Eraser (a big pink one)
- Screw-holding screwdriver
- Note pad and graph paper
- Long-nose pliers
- Chalk line pickup tool
- Magnet
- 12-foot tape measure
- 10-inch tweezers
- Sandpaper and block
- Cutting pliers (needle nose)
- Crescent wrench
- Wire stripper
- Slip-joint pliers
- Electrician's knife
- Needle-nose pliers
- Nut driver
- Standard slot screwdriver
- Soldering gun or iron
- Solder (60 percent tin and 40 percent lead)
- Wood glue
- Rosin flux
- Duct tape
- Neon test lamp
- Electrician's tape
- Masking tape
- C-clamp
- Rubber or plastic mallet
- Tack hammer
- 16-ounce curved-claw hammer
- Miter box
- Backsaw
- Crosscut saw
- Torpedo level
- Combination square
- Utility knife with extra blades in handle
- Pocketknife
- Whetstone
- Saber saw
- Power drill with adapter for driving wallboard screws

Paint
- 1½-inch natural-hair paintbrush
- 4-inch synthetic-bristle paintbrush
- Sash brush
- Painting pad and edger
- Roller and roller cover
- Plastic tray liner
- Sponge brushes
- Steel wool
- Plastic gloves
- Drop cloth or tarp

Plumbing
- 3-inch plunger
- Bucket
- Hex wrench
- Basin wrench
- 1- to 1½-inch tube cutter
- No. 1 spool or 50/50 solid solder
- 2-ounce can of soldering paste
- Pipe joint compound
- Stiff brush for spreading
- Plumber's wicking
- Plumber's putty
- Propane torch

Wallboard
- Jigsaw points
- Glaze compound
- Vises
- Glass cutter
- 12-inch drill press
- 5-inch putty knife
- Graft knives
- Wallboard knife with 11-inch blade
- Glue gun
- Sticks roller
- Assorted hardware
- Cup hooks
- Eyebolts and screw eyes
- Wallboard screws
- Box nails, brads, and finishing nails
- Expansion screws

A CLOSET WORKSHOP

Another small space that can be turned into a workshop is a closet. Here are some questions to ask yourself: Should you divide the wall space? Will extra shelves be useful? What about the floor space? Will crates or caddies work here? Can things be hung or stored on the back of the door?

Different Kinds of Closets

The standard bedroom or hall closet offers considerable space for storing tools. The back of the door or doors can be used for shelving. The type that is attached by brackets or hung over the door itself will go up quickly. A pegboard can accommodate hand tools. A folding or roll-out workbench may fit into the closet. You might build a fold-down bench top right into the door, not unlike a built-in ironing board. Be sure that it is enough for the work that you plan to do.

If the closet has no shelves, add some. Depending on the side of the closet, one or two shelves 10 to 12 inches deep would be useful. Graduate the depth of the shelves above them so that you can see and reach all the way to the ceiling.

You could divide the back wall of the closet in half and put pegboard on one side and shelving on the other. Consider adding a metal cabinet if you are using toxics. If you want a light that pulls out of the closet, install an accordion-style reading lamp. With imagination you can use many of these ideas to convert other types of closets. Plans for any closet should include a work surface, shelves for storage, a closed hanging or standing cabinet, an inside light, and a pegboard for hanging tools.

The space under the basement stairs may also be a real find. There is usually less traffic in this area, so you can leave the workshop open. Here you can build in a full cabinet with all the shelves and compartments you want, add a pegboard, and install an overhead lamp and a workbench.

Components of a Closet Workshop

If the closet door does not allow easy access, consider removing the existing door and replacing it with an accordion-fold door or with bifold louvers. You can then open the closet.

A metal filing cabinet and a ¾-inch plywood top can be combined to create a work surface. Alternatively, you might build a workbench. Look over some of the portable or smaller units discussed in the fourth chapter.

Try to keep materials and tools at the bench. Running around gathering supplies wastes time. If the shop is in a small space, it may be necessary to have lumber and plywood cut to size at the lumberyard. Then you can bring it back all ready to assemble.

Understairs Workshop

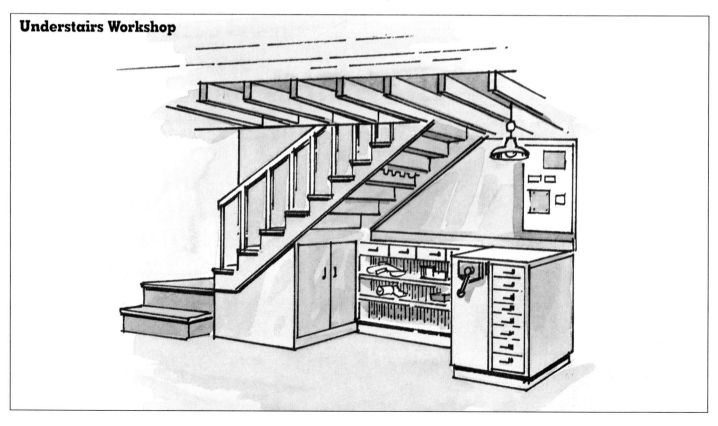

Closet Workshop

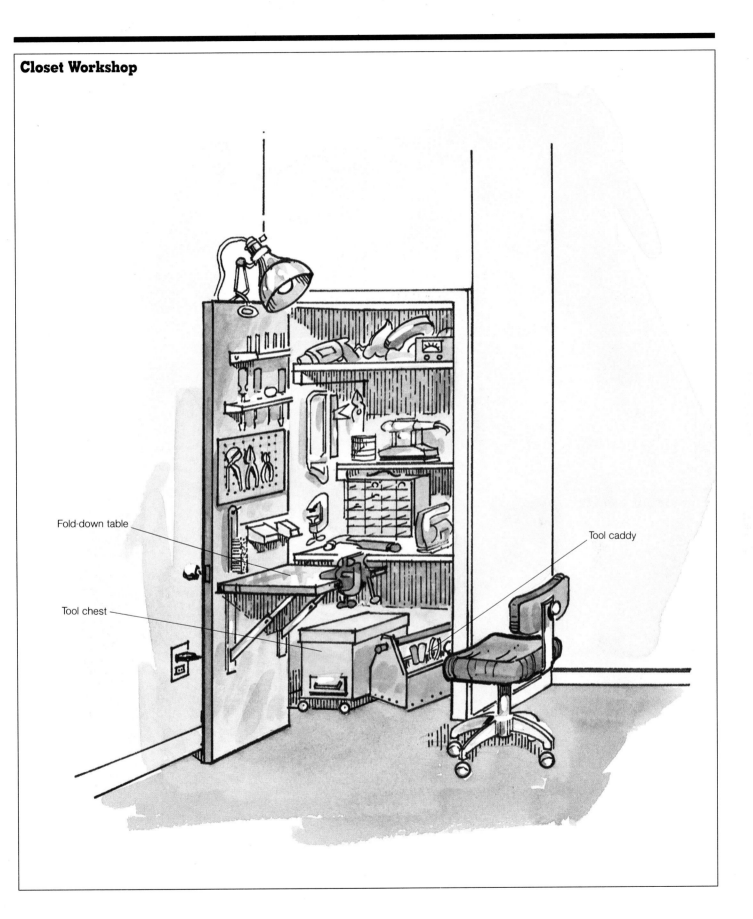

Fold-down table

Tool chest

Tool caddy

Roll-Out Closet Workbench

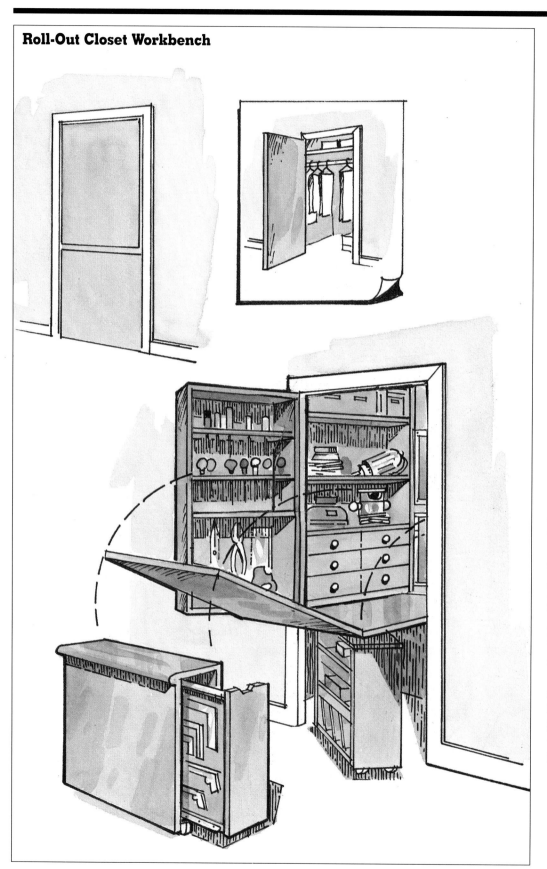

The Roll-Out Workbench

Almost any closet can accommodate a roll-out bench that includes storage space for tools and materials. Just open the door and trundle out the whole shop. Choose a closet located where traffic won't disturb work in progress, perhaps in a spare room.

Tools in the Closet

Thinking small means thinking basic when it comes to tools. Don't neglect the essential power tools, but concentrate on hand tools.

Add Storage With Furniture

Built for sturdiness, an old bureau or armoire can be used to store materials or hand tools. It can even double as a workbench. Place it near the closet to extend the available space. If you refinish it, no one will know that this attractive piece of furniture is really a home workshop.

The drawers of a large armoire might hold power tools. A pegboard for hand tools and jars and totes for hardware can be hung inside the doors. A portable workbench might fit between the shelves; if not, it is easily stored behind the piece.

An old schoolteacher's desk makes an excellent bench for handcrafts or electrical work. Loaded with drawers and dividers, it is perfect for storing tools, kits, and supplies.

The Tool Armoire

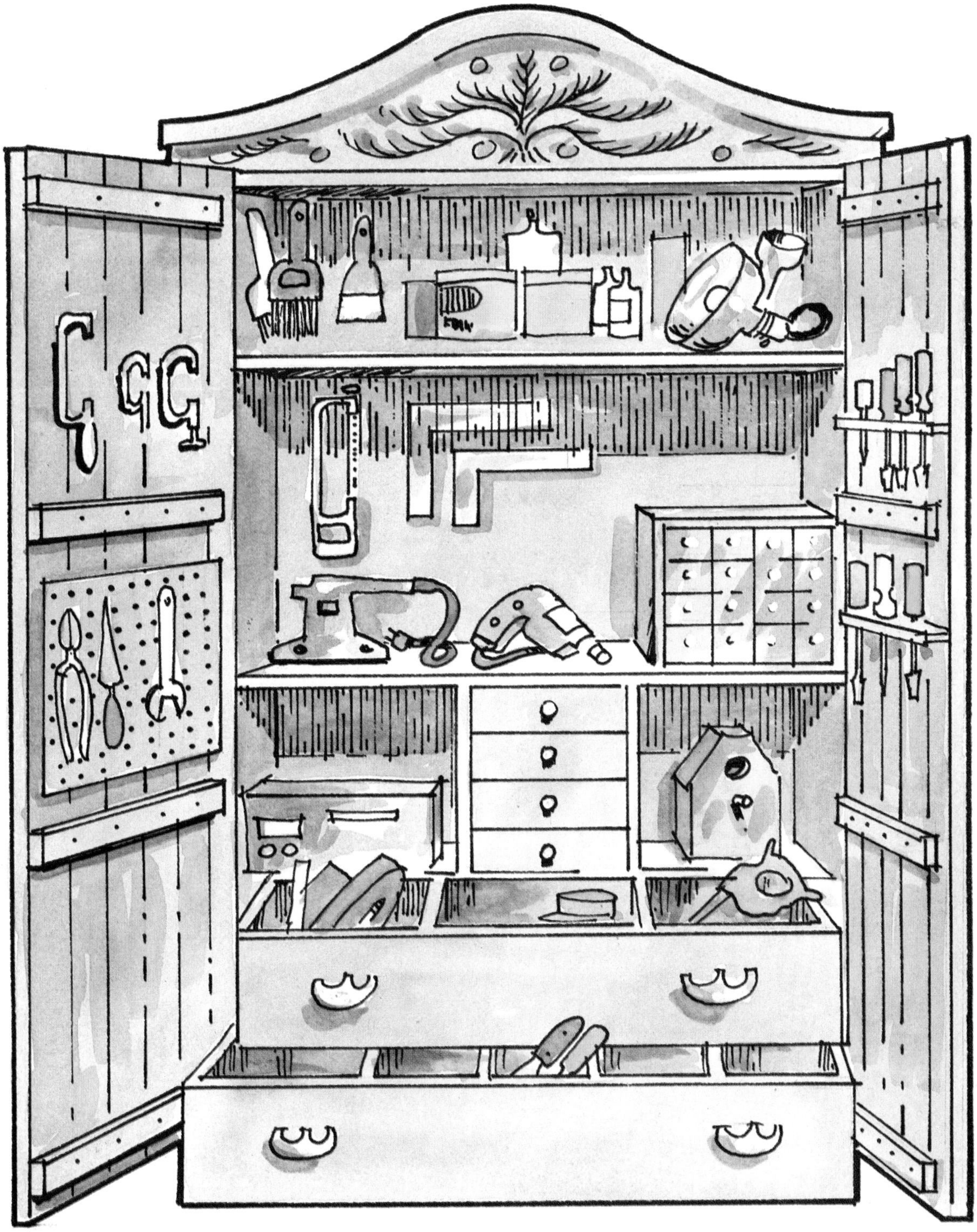

AN APARTMENT OR CONDO WORKSHOP

Living in an apartment or owning a condominium doesn't preclude having a home workshop. It simply means that you will need to do more planning. Going over the plans with the neighbor next door is a must. Should there be a problem, rethink your plan to resolve any potential conflict.

In an apartment or a condo, you might have a spare room, or part of one, or a closet to use as a workshop. Read through the section on closets and consider the application of some of the ideas and suggestions to your spare room.

Although hand tools will be the mainstay of an apartment workshop, include a few stationary power pieces on the wish list. Depending on noise level and on the wall area, you may be able to use a drill press, for example, in a small room. If you do woodworking, noise will be a problem. If your spare room shares a wall (a party wall) with a neighboring apartment, be sure that noisy machines are not placed against or too close to the wall.

Make certain that your apartment or condo is adequately wired for the tools you plan to use. Investigate the effect of large tools on radio and TV.

Many apartments are built with a linen closet opposite a spare room. This closet could be designated to store the tools that are used in the workshop across the hall. Again, be sure that they are organized in a way that makes them easy to transport.

A kitchen corner in an apartment may be small, but consider the suggestions for hanging things in closets. Apply some of these ideas to the wall space near one cabinet to make a nice niche for working. Don't think small just because you are living in a small area.

Spare Room Layouts

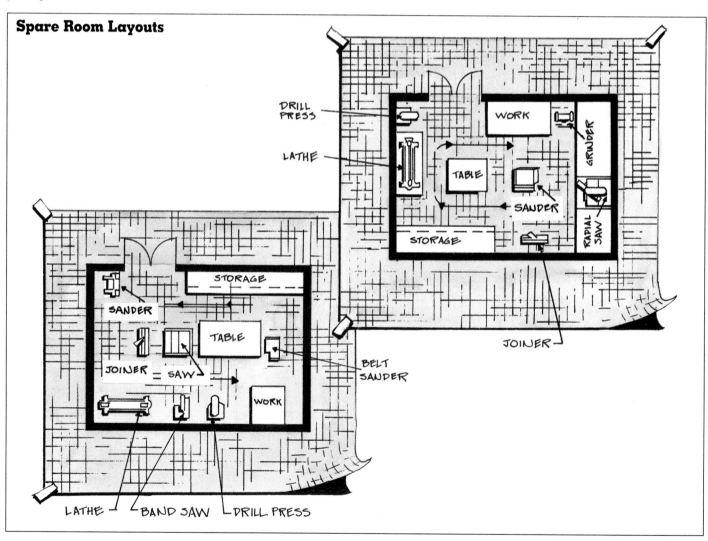

THE ATTIC

Ventilation is a must in the attic workshop. With proper ventilation and temperature control, the attic can be a good choice—but there are other issues to consider as well.

Questions That Need Answers

Take a good, hard look at the attic before you establish a shop there. Above all, look at the pitch of the roof. Will there be enough headroom over your workbench? If you can't stand up comfortably, forget it. However, if there are places where you can work standing, or if all of your work will be done sitting down, use your ingenuity to find work space and storage space. Ask yourself the following questions.

Is There Enough Space?

Start by measuring the floor area and the height of the ceiling. Do they meet code requirements? Check the local code. The ceiling should be at least 7 feet high over 50 percent of the floor space in an attic. Remember that you may be moving large, unwieldy objects around. Calculate well; will you have enough room to move comfortably from one job to another?

Is There Enough Headroom?

If the attic doesn't have enough headroom, consider enlarging it. This can also give more floor space. Some attics can be easily enlarged; others will be more difficult and expensive. Your budget may decide this question for you. If you are planning a major renovation, consider adding a dormer. This will give you a window, more wall space, and more headroom. Always have a professional contractor, engineer, or architect look at the house before you undertake any structural changes.

Is the Floor Strong Enough?

If the attic is floored, check the joists. If they are designed for a light load, they will have to be reinforced. Measure the spacing between the joists. Use this information to decide whether your floor will be strong enough to support any heavy machines or projects that are in your plans. If you are in any doubt, get professional advice.

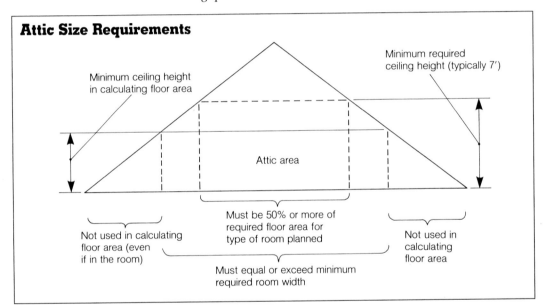

Attic Size Requirements

Minimum ceiling height in calculating floor area

Minimum required ceiling height (typically 7')

Attic area

Not used in calculating floor area (even if in the room)

Must be 50% or more of required floor area for type of room planned

Not used in calculating floor area

Must equal or exceed minimum required room width

Floor Joists

Allowable spans for 40 pounds per square foot live load. Listed in feet and inches. OC means inches on center.

Joist Size	Joist Spacing	Modules of Elasticity, E, in 1,000,000 psi													
		0.8	0.9	1.0	1.1	1.2	1.3	1.4	1.5	1.6	1.7	1.8	1.9	2.0	2.2
2×6	16 OC	7-9	8-0	8-4	8-4	8-10	9-1	9-4	9-6	9-9	9-11	10-2	10-4	10-6	10-10
	24 OC	6-9	7-0	7-3	7-6	7-9	7-11	8-2	8-4	8-6	8-8	8-10	9-0	9-2	9-6
2×8	16 OC	10-2	10-7	11-0	11-4	11-8	12-0	12-3	12-7	12-10	13-1	13-4	13-7	13-10	14-3
	24 OC	8-11	9-3	9-7	9-11	10-2	10-6	10-9	11-0	11-3	11-5	11-8	11-11	12-1	12-6
2×10	16 OC	13-0	13-6	14-0	14-6	14-11	15-3	15-8	16-0	16-5	16-9	17-0	17-4	17-8	18-3
	24 OC	11-4	11-10	12-3	12-8	13-0	13-4	13-8	14-0	14-4	14-7	14-11	15-2	15-5	15-11
2×12	16 OC	15-10	16-5	17-0	17-7	18-1	18-7	19-1	19-6	19-11	20-4	20-9	21-1	21-6	22-2
	24 OC	13-10	14-4	14-11	15-4	15-10	16-3	16-8	17-0	17-5	17-9	18-1	18-5	18-9	19-4

Adapted from the 1991 edition of the Uniform Building Code.

If the joists are adequate, you can lay plywood sheathing over them. This will provide a comfortable floor. You might want to add indoor-outdoor carpet for noise control and insulation.

Is Access Adequate?

You need to get to the attic. If there is a stairway, is it too steep or narrow to be practical? Could you carry tools and materials up the stairs?

If there is no stairway, you will have to hire a professional to design one. This is a big project, and it requires specialized knowledge. Consider too that stairs take up a lot of space. A simple straight-run stairway requires almost 50 square feet of floor area downstairs and 35 to 40 square feet upstairs. This is almost like taking a whole room out of use. You will certainly lose some of the space that you were planning to use for other purposes. Carefully check through the whole plan again.

Fold-away stairs are easily installed. This might be the answer if there is no stairway, provided that your projects will be small. You cannot carry large objects up and down these stairs. Consider the space above and below when deciding where to place the unit. Here too you will remove some space from the floor plan of the shop. Finally, consider where the dust and fumes will go when the attic is opened into the main house.

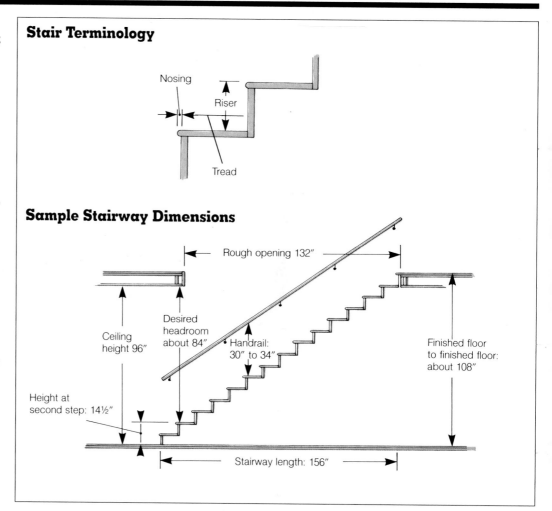

Stair Terminology

Sample Stairway Dimensions

Are There Obstructions?

Most unfinished attics are full of pipes, flues, vents, chimneys, and framing members. These can be annoying obstacles. Some of them can be moved or taken out altogether. The rest must be incorporated into the storage units or left exposed.

Movables include small plumbing vents, heating ducts, and small flues. These can be rerouted. Immovable objects include chimneys, large flues and plumbing vents, and the posts that support the ridge beam. If you are leaving these exposed,

decorate the rest of the shop to match. Painting the duct work bright, attractive colors can look high tech.

Build around obstructions. Add a plywood panel or a pegboard under the eaves to hang tools on. Behind the panel you could create storage space to the very bottom of the roof run. When building an obstruction into a unit, be aware of the clearance for combustibles, and check the local code to ensure a safe design.

Is There Enough Light?

The attic may have one small window, or none. Skylights and overhead windows can add to the natural lighting. However, in order to provide the strong light that you will need, mount fluorescent or incandescent fixtures on the ridge beam or the walls. Allow for at least two long shop lamps. Make sure that the whole shop is well lit; corners that remain dark won't be used. Track lighting is inexpensive, and because each lamp is movable you can put the light exactly where you want it. Painting the roof space a pale color will also increase the illumination.

Heat Circulation

Insulation

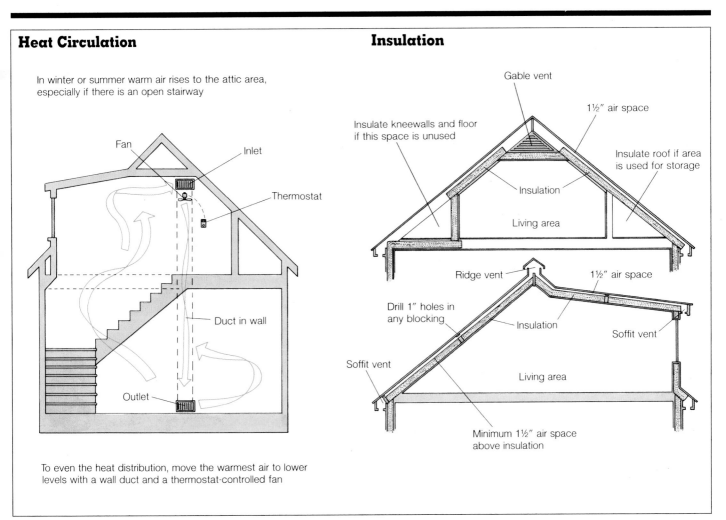

In winter or summer warm air rises to the attic area, especially if there is an open stairway

Fan

Inlet

Thermostat

Duct in wall

Outlet

To even the heat distribution, move the warmest air to lower levels with a wall duct and a thermostat-controlled fan

Gable vent

1½" air space

Insulate kneewalls and floor if this space is unused

Insulate roof if area is used for storage

Insulation

Living area

Ridge vent

1½" air space

Drill 1" holes in any blocking

Insulation

Soffit vent

Soffit vent

Living area

Minimum 1½" air space above insulation

Is There Enough Ventilation?

Attics need fresh air. If there is a window, the typical code requirement for the opening is 1/20 of the floor area of the room or at least 5 square feet. A skylight will also let in fresh air. Placing a window and a skylight opposite each other would provide good cross-ventilation.

There are probably louvers at the ends of the house. Adding an exhaust fan here might be fairly easy. See the illustration on page 29 and adapt it to the available wall space. According to most codes any ventilation device that is installed must provide at least one fresh-air exchange per hour.

Is Wiring Adequate?

You will need at least one general-purpose circuit, a switch by the door that controls a light or outlet, and at least one outlet for each wall. Be sure that the stairway is well lit. A subpanel that can be locked is a good safety feature for an attic wiring system.

Although you can add to the existing wiring, it is far better to install a new circuit for the workshop. Be sure that a licensed electrician does this work or inspects it after you do it.

Smoke detectors should be installed in any workshop. Wiring them into the house circuit is easier than remembering to get batteries later.

Can the Space Be Heated?

Most attic shops have electric baseboard heat or a small gas heater. Probably you will seldom use them, since the attic retains so much heat from the rest of the house. For really cold spells you may want to extend the duct work from the central heating system. Consider too that you are close to the roof, and you have the chimney available. A small wood-burning stove could take care of those occasional freezing spells. Check the local code before pursuing any of these ideas.

Attic Workshop Layout

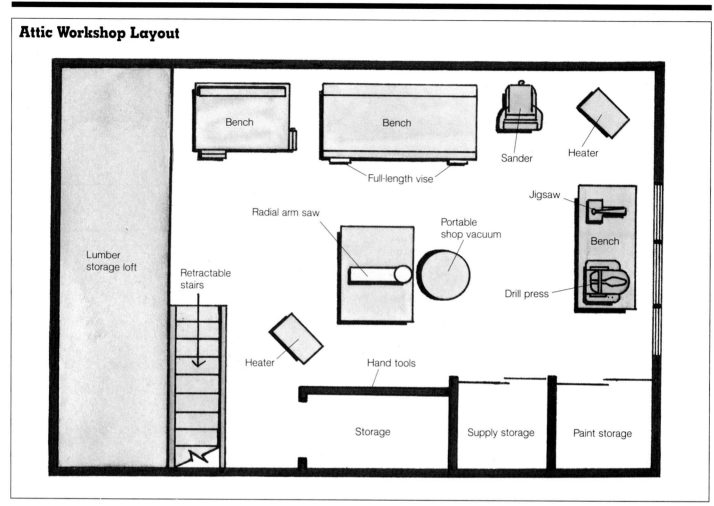

Lumber storage loft

Retractable stairs

Bench

Bench

Full-length vise

Sander

Heater

Jigsaw

Bench

Drill press

Radial arm saw

Portable shop vacuum

Heater

Hand tools

Storage

Supply storage

Paint storage

Can the Space Be Cooled?

An attic fan will keep the shop cool in summer. It will also cool the entire house, and it will move heat from lower floors to the attic during the winter. Insulation is another option. Again, consult the local code for specifics.

Can the Space Be Kept Dust Free?

Since the attic is above the rest of the house, a shop vacuum is a necessity. The dust filtering down or carried out on your clothes and shoes can create a mess downstairs. When the attic has no window, keeping the shop clean will keep the air cleaner too.

Can Noise Be Kept to a Minimum?

Think now about ways to stop noise from traveling through the attic floor. Fire-retardant wall rugs were discussed on page 28. Placing such sound-deadening panels over the joists and under the subfloor also works. Install a so-called floating floor—fiberglass blankets laid directly over the subfloor and covered with the finish floor of your choice. Weather stripping around the door will keep both noise and dust out too.

Planning the Attic Workshop

Now that you have examined the problems posed by your particular attic, it's time to plan the workshop you are going to build there.

In an attic with low headroom, use both sides for storage; the bench and the stationary power tools can be placed in the center of the floor. The radial arm saw in the illustration is partially enclosed by a hood, which connects to a portable shop vacuum.

Finding Storage Space

The kneewalls, those short sidewalls in an attic, contain a lot of storage space. This is the place to build recessed shelves. You might even install a bench that you could sit at to utilize this area. If there are no kneewalls in your attic, build cabinets, drawer units, or low closets into the angle where the roof meets the floor. This is a good way to extend the room. Make one of the storage units accessible from the side and give yourself a long wall for mounting hand tools. If you don't want to build shelves, use crates or stacking boxes.

The Attic Roofline

Account for headroom clearance over work and storage areas

Hanging things from the roof beams works fine for a simple shop. Keep headroom and clearance in mind. Build shelves into the spans of the rafters to make use of the existing structure. Remember that some of this shelving should be closed to provide storage for toxics or chemicals.

Keep large stationary tools to a minimum in this restricted space. Weight is an important consideration. Put the kit idea into effect by designating shelves for various caddies. The storage bins beneath the eaves can even be color coded for better organization.

Placing Workbenches

A self-contained workbench with a tool well like the one described on page 15 could be adapted for the attic. Keep it tucked under the eaves and roll it out to use in the open center space of the attic. It could hold all your tools and include a power source as well.

Workbenches for the attic will be built against a high wall, if there is one, or in the center of the room. In the latter case, mount some of the power tools on the bench. A turning turret will accommodate as many as four different power tools. This makes it possible to utilize the middle of the workbench top, which is often empty otherwise.

The lumber that you need for your projects may be bought precut, or you may be lucky enough to have space for a lumber loft.

IDSIZE WORKSHOPS

It's been said that workshops aren't planned; they just happen. Most often they happen in a garage or basement. In fact, however, you really need to plan extensively for these locations. You will be sharing space with the car, the furnace, the water heater, and perhaps the washer and dryer. You also need to think through the time schedules of your fellow users. If the workshop is carefully planned, conflict with other users can be mitigated or avoided entirely. Careful planning will also eliminate conflicts over space use (the washing machine and band saw won't be vying for the same spot on the floor).

If you plan to make extensive changes, consider the impact on the house or garage should you later decide to sell. As much as possible, allow for the dismantling of the workshop. A prospective buyer might not share your euphoria over a workshop in the basement where there used to be a complete family room!

The workshop in this two-car garage has been well planned. Because the shop must share the space with the family car, all of the machines and the workbench have been mounted on wheels so that each can be moved into position when needed and stored out of the way when not in use.

THE GARAGE

A garage makes a good workshop, because it keeps noise and mess well away from the house. Build a carport to keep the car in and you can have the whole garage for a shop. You might even extend one side of the garage and build a bay underneath it for storage.

Vertical and Horizontal Storage

Open stud walls provide vertical as well as horizontal space for storage. The area above the hood of the car is ordinarily wasted. If the garage is small, build shelves or lockers in this area. Remember to allow plenty of clearance. Hammocks designed for storing toys work well for holding paint rollers, clean rags, and other soft stashables slung over the hood.

The rafters can provide storage for ladders or lumber. Store automotive supplies in containers on shelves secured to the studs with wallboard screws. Hang pegboards on one wall for tools. Keep combustibles and toxics in a locked metal cabinet.

Built-in floor-to-ceiling wall lockers and the small built-in desk under the window take excellent advantage of available space.

Storing Lumber

Horizontal Lumber Storage

Vertical Lumber Storage

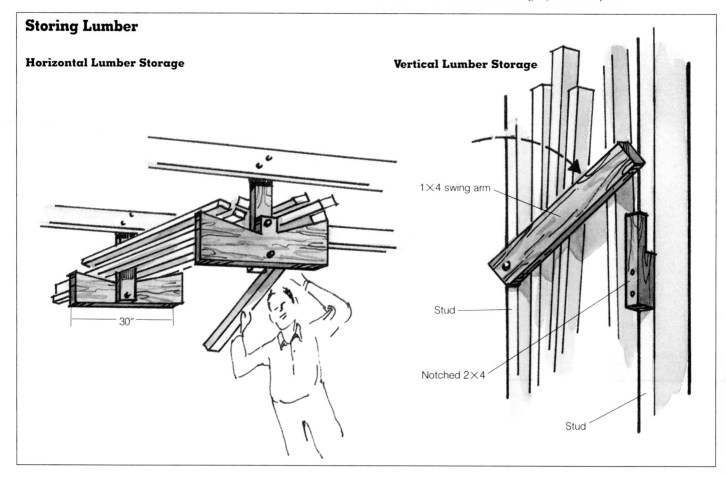

30"

1×4 swing arm

Stud

Notched 2×4

Stud

Garage Workshop

Allow for the Car

When the car is going to be kept in the garage, make sure that there will be room to move it in and out. Remember to leave space for opening the doors, trunk, and hood. If you are storing things over the hood, be sure that these things can be moved easily.

People who enjoy working on cars transform their garages into auto shops. A bench across the back wall provides a work area, and the space below it accommodates awkward items—tires, a dolly, even an engine block awaiting repair.

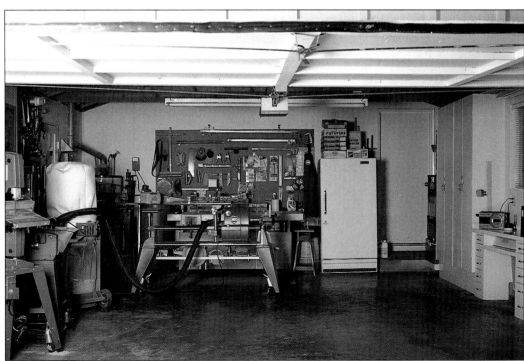

Mounted on wheels, the machines and the workbench have been pushed back to make room for the car.

Shelves in the Garage

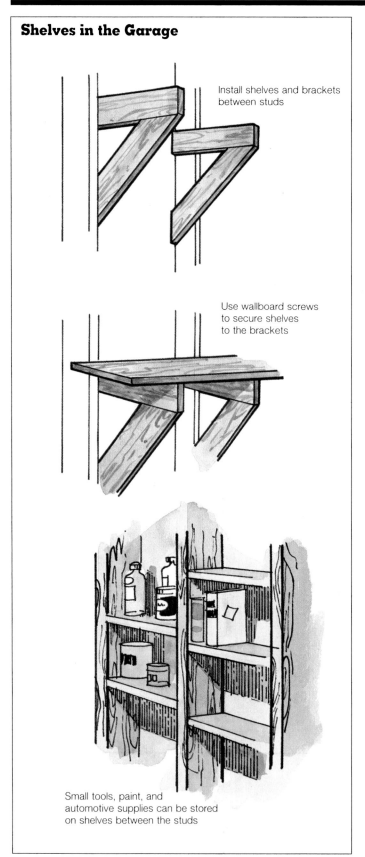

Install shelves and brackets between studs

Use wallboard screws to secure shelves to the brackets

Small tools, paint, and automotive supplies can be stored on shelves between the studs

Windows and Doors

Take advantage of any windows in the garage. They will provide strong natural light, but be sure to avoid glare; don't place equipment so that you must work with the sun in your eyes. Control the light with shades or blinds if necessary. Place your bench under the window and use the sills to hold small tools and containers of nails. Try not to block the windows themselves by storing things in front of them. A fine view adds to the joy of a window workbench.

Carefully plan the placement of major tools. If you put the table saw near the garage door, you will be able to cut large pieces of lumber with the door open. Putting large free-standing tools on wheels or into carts will enable you to store them away from the work area and move them into position when you need them. This means that you can use the driveway for planing or cutting very large boards. Use tarps to collect sawdust and shavings; these can damage the lawn. Sawdust can be used to soak up fluids used for automotive repair, especially antifreeze, which can poison your pets.

An overhead door may be left open most of the time, but you should note its clearance on the floor plan. When you organize the garage, be careful not to block the movement of the door.

Lighting

The old standby double-tube fluorescent light is inexpensive and still as effective as ever. Replace the standard 13-inch cord with a longer one so it can be moved around the shop without having to unplug it.

A light that can be clamped to the bench is very helpful for doing woodworking or intricate projects such as stained glass. Mount a board at the rear of the workbench and clamp the light anywhere along it.

A retractable reel lamp solves many lighting problems. Mount it on the ceiling or wall and pull it out whenever you need it. When you've finished, give it a tug and back it goes into its housing.

Electrical Outlets

If you are planning to add new circuits in the garage, consult a professional electrician. An all-purpose wiring layout might include a subpanel near the door to feed one circuit through a switch to a fluorescent light above the workbench. Another circuit could power a string of outlets along the back of the bench, an overhead outlet on a reel system, and a standard wall outlet. A third circuit could power outlets located near stationary equipment. One of these could be a floor outlet for a table saw. All circuit cables should be encased in steel conduit. The circuit breaker for the fluorescent

This garage workshop takes advantage of its overhead space. Note the permanent pipe installation of the dust removal system, the racks for plywood and lumber storage, the retractable electric power cords, and the rolled-back overhead door.

Clamp-On Swing-Arm Lamp

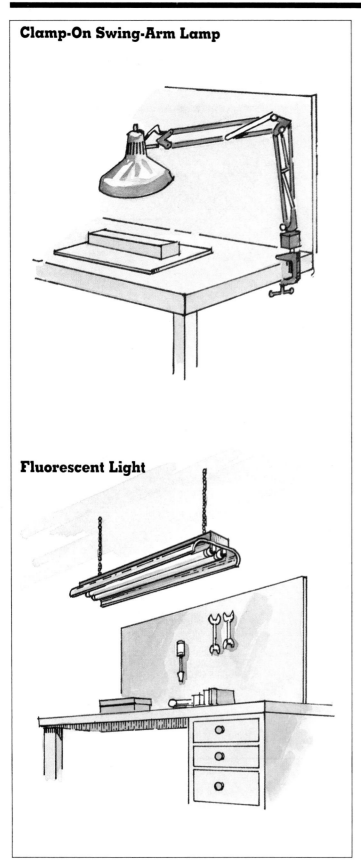

Fluorescent Light

Central Heat

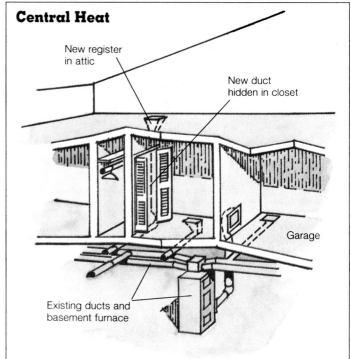

New register in attic

New duct hidden in closet

Garage

Existing ducts and basement furnace

light will probably be left on. The breakers for the other two circuits can be shut off to keep children from playing with the power tools.

Always be sure to install the best quality ground fault circuit interrupters (GFCIs). There are two models—one protects itself and the circuit it is wired through; the other acts as a circuit breaker to protect the entire line. Either model will detect current leak and cut off the circuit in a quarter of a second. Be sure to match the size of the circuit wire to the capacity of the breaker. For 15-ampere lighting circuits, use No. 14 copper wire; for 20-ampere portable-power-tool circuits, use No. 12 wire; for 20-ampere heavy-duty 240-volt circuits, use No. 12 wire.

Temperature Control

Insulation will keep the garage cooler in summer and warmer in winter. If you plan to heat the shop, find out whether the ventilation is adequate and whether you will need a chimney. Duct work from the existing furnace could be used for heating if the garage is connected to the house. Think about efficiency, though, before you bore the hole. In mild climates space heating is often enough. In cold climates insulation and a wood-burning stove may be the answer. Check the local building and fire codes before you install such a stove in the garage, and remember that you will need heat shields and a place to store fuel.

Many garages get intensely hot in the summer. A large window fan or floor fan may help some, but a window air conditioner would be better.

THE FREESTANDING BUILDING

Many styles and sizes of freestanding structures can be bought at most lumberyards. If you are handy at carpentry, you may want to build your own shed to use as a workshop.

The Shed

Sheds make perfect workshops. They offer easy access for materials and plenty of storage for tools and lumber. Because the shed is separate from the house, you can just lock it up and leave half-finished projects inside.

Draw Up a Site Plan

Sketch a site plan of the property. Include everything from the bushes to the dog run.

Include the inside plan of the house too, and the windows and doors. How will the shed affect the view from these windows? Noises from the new shop will be heard in nearby rooms. All of these factors will influence the placement of the building.

On the plan note possible problem areas, such as the placement of the barbecue, or the trash cans. This will help

you to focus on how you use the yard. Where you find things is where the whole family actually uses them, whether it's practical or not. The shed should have its own place, out of the way of other activities.

Codes and Permits

Before you erect any structure, you must contact the local building inspection office. They might send someone to look over the site, which could help you with the planning. The building codes will specify proper construction standards for your community. It will also specify the distance required between buildings and adjacent property lines.

Labor and Cost

How much work will it take to build your own shed? There is a lot of time and effort involved, so be realistic. Many home-improvement centers will install the kit sheds that they sell. Most of these come with complete materials and instructions. The more complicated ones are usually more difficult to construct. Prices range from roughly $150 to $800; wood sheds are more expensive than metal ones. Extras include site preparation, anchors for the metal shed, a pad for either, and anything else you might want that is not part of the package.

Freestanding Shed

Site Map

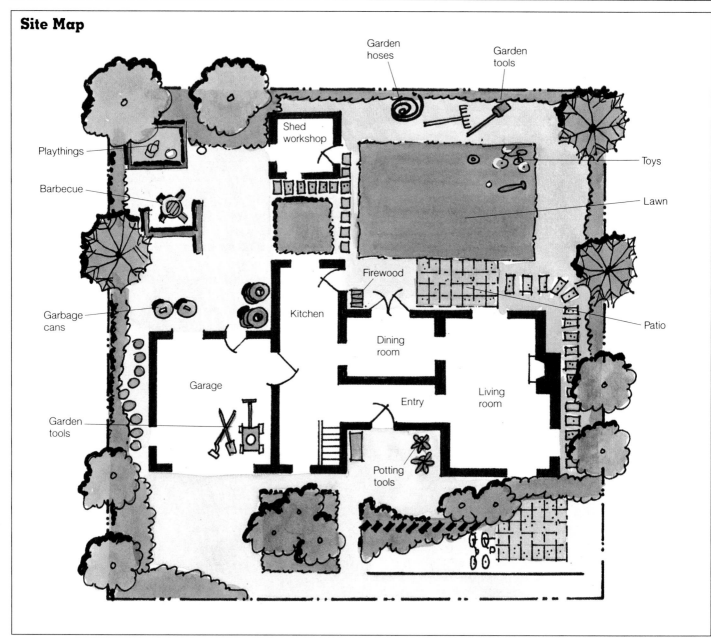

Garden hoses

Garden tools

Playthings

Barbecue

Shed workshop

Toys

Lawn

Firewood

Garbage cans

Kitchen

Dining room

Patio

Garden tools

Garage

Entry

Living room

Potting tools

The Site

The building site helps to determine the size of the shed and the time needed to erect the structure. The site should be easy to reach in all types of weather, and by people who are carrying large, heavy objects. Think too about how you will go to and from the shed. Will this new traffic pattern affect any other? Will it damage the lawn? Will the shed displace other important activities?

Sun and Shadow

Locate the shed to take advantage of solar energy for heat and light. It is best if the longest wall faces south, but be aware of the shadows that the shed will cast. Will plantings in the garden be affected?

View

Will the shed dominate its surroundings? Will it block a view from the house or from a neighbor's house?

Terrain

The best spot will be flat, firm, and dry, so that the building can sit square, settle evenly, and drain naturally. Building on a slope is more difficult and usually requires the services of a professional. Soft ground will not settle well, and damp ground will shorten the life of the shed. This is important—moisture will damage all of your tools as well as the structure itself.

Typical Metal Shed Assembly

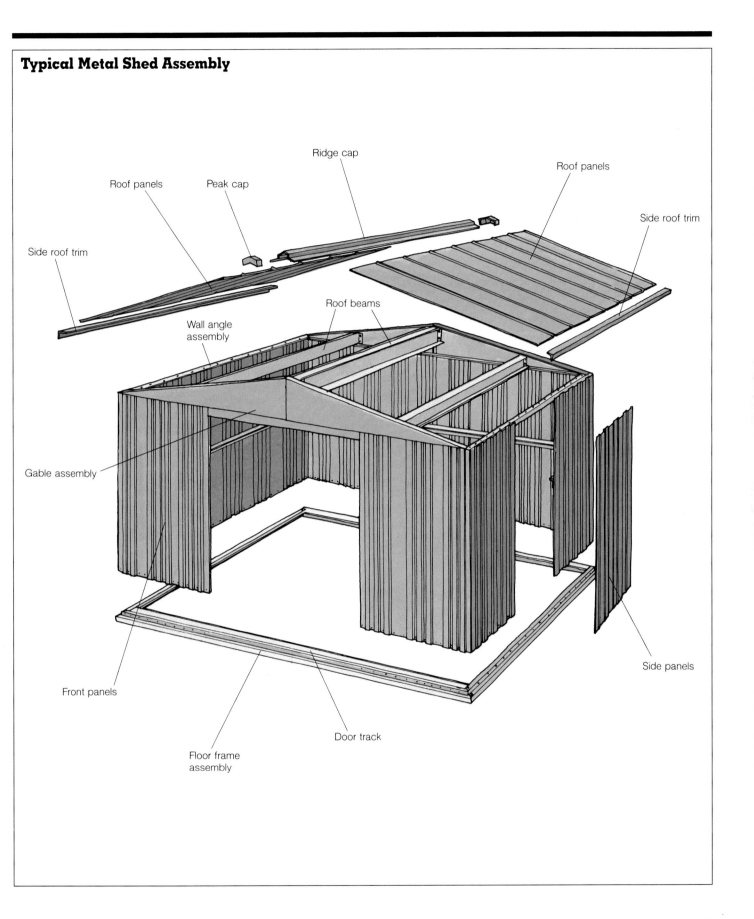

Ridge cap

Roof panels

Peak cap

Roof panels

Side roof trim

Side roof trim

Roof beams

Wall angle assembly

Gable assembly

Front panels

Floor frame assembly

Door track

Side panels

A Kit is a Package of Parts

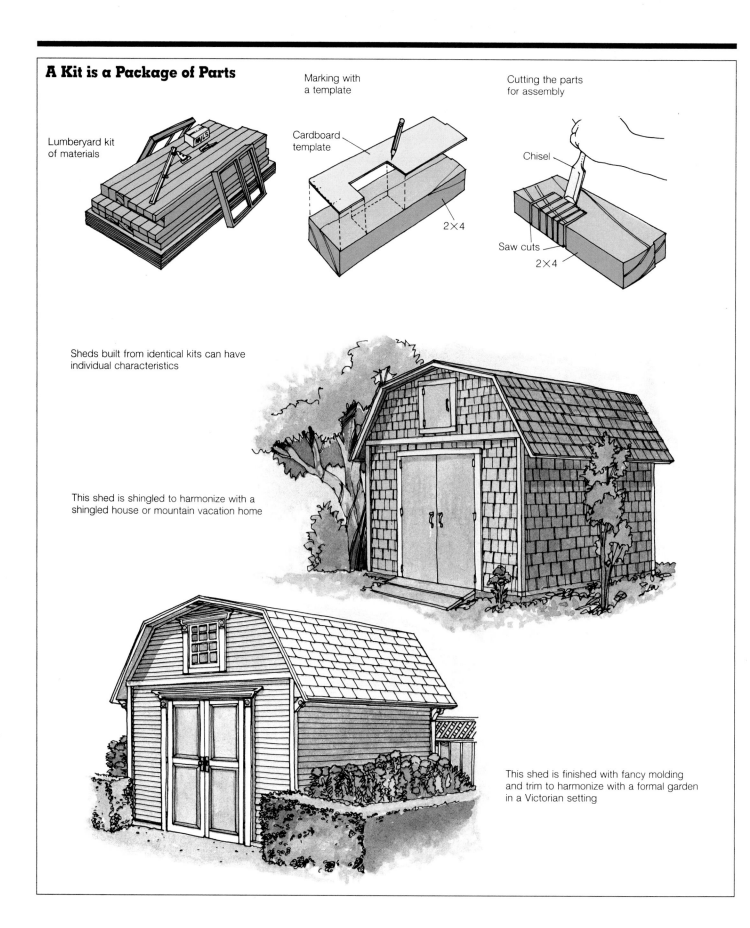

Marking with
a template

Cutting the parts
for assembly

Lumberyard kit
of materials

Cardboard
template

Chisel

2×4

Saw cuts

2×4

Sheds built from identical kits can have
individual characteristics

This shed is shingled to harmonize with a
shingled house or mountain vacation home

This shed is finished with fancy molding
and trim to harmonize with a formal garden
in a Victorian setting

Top: A freestanding workshop
building has many advantages.
Perhaps the most important is that
it keeps noise and dust out of the
living quarters.
Bottom: This freestanding pool
house converted to a workshop can
easily be converted back if the home
is sold to new owners who aren't
do-it-yourselfers.

Climate and Moisture

Choose a building that is appropriate for the climate. A metal shed in particular is susceptible to damage from strong winds, heavy snows, and salt air. If you live near the seacoast, pick an aluminum product over a steel one. Keep snow and ice from accumulating on the roof. Excessive moisture rots wood sheds. Keep wetness out of either type of shed. If you live in an area that has frequent high winds it needs to be tied down securely.

If you live in an area where the ground freezes, the building may be prone to movement. Stationary power equipment may operate poorly, or not at all, on an unlevel surface. Foundation footings should sit on solid earth below the frost line. A surface foundation, such as piers without footings, will be subject to frost heave, since piers sit on the earth, not in it.

Heat can make a small shed very uncomfortable. Combined with moisture it can encourage the growth of fungus and mildew. Install a window or vents in the gables if you live in a hot climate. Foundation vents will bring cross-ventilation into the shed.

Water is the enemy of workshops. A shed is particularly affected at the top and bottom. If it is built on a concrete slab, a sheet of 6-mil plastic between the slab and the earth will serve as a vapor barrier. The roof should slope enough to allow the easy runoff of rain, and the site should be graded so that any runoff will flow away from the building. A good pitch will allow snow to slide off too. The overhang should be wide enough so that runoff will not fall on the foundation. A shingled roof needs more pitch than one that is covered with roll roofing. Each joint or break represents a potential leak. Use flashing, caulk, and sealants to make the shed watertight.

Windows and Doors

If you build your own shed, you can design the placement of the windows. If you buy a prefabricated unit, choose one that has enough windows to take maximum advantage of natural light. Skylights provide ventilation and light and enable you to make better use of wall space.

A shed with doors at each end is ideal. However, two doors on one end will also give good access for large objects. Mount the doors off center to leave more wall space for tools and storage.

Electricity

If the shed is located near the house, using heavy-duty extension cord or an outside outlet can provide enough electricity for a small shop. On the other hand, if you intend to use many power tools the shed should be completely wired by a professional electrician.

Opposite: Filtered natural light
suffuses a shed workshop
constructed of fiberglass or
plastic panels.
Top and bottom: A bank of clear
glass windows brings direct natural
light into the work area.

This converted freestanding pool house is conveniently located a short distance from the main house on firm, level terrain. The double doors let in a lot of natural light and provide access for large projects. The interior has plenty of space for benches and machines, tool storage, and even a place to watch a ball game.

Wood Sheds Versus Metal Sheds

Once you have chosen a spot for the shed, think about the type of structure you will place there. Whether you purchase a prefabricated shed or build your own, you will probably want it to harmonize with the style and color of the house. If you decide to buy a prefabricated unit, you must choose between metal and wood. This is an important choice, since each material has its own functions and attributes.

	Wood	Metal
Materials	Structural lumber (occasionally steel) framing pieces. Exterior siding of plywood, particleboard, waferboard, or other sheathing material. Materials vary from dealer to dealer.	Usually galvanized steel with heavy-duty enamel finish. Sometimes aluminum. Look for sheds with American Society for Testing and Materials (A.S.T.M.) approval.
Completeness of kit	Varies considerably; few kits supply all materials.	All needed parts are supplied except foundation anchors. Flooring is an option; it is not always available.
Cost	From $350 to $3,000, depending on the size of the structure and the type and quality of materials provided. Foundation materials are often extra.	Generally $300 to $1,000, depending on size and special features. Anchoring and site preparation are extra.
Time and tools required to install	Varies according to the skill of the builder and the scope of the project; usually several days. Full complement of carpentry tools, in many cases.	One day or less. Screwdriver, pliers, stepladder, plus tools for site preparation are provided; selection varies according to the type of foundation chosen.
Skills needed to install	Good carpentry skills are very helpful and in some cases essential.	Relatively few skills needed.
Possibility for exterior modification	Dimensions and design features can often be modified to meet individual needs. Customized look is easy to create with finish materials, paint, and trim.	Slight—dimensions and appearance are predetermined. Some manufacturers sell optional window kits.
Possibility for outfitting interior	Interiors are easily outfitted with built-in structures or wall-mounted components.	Limited options; accessories are available from some manufacturers.
Disadvantages of the material	Subject to rot if exterior-grade materials are not used. Any wood that contacts the ground should be pressure treated.	Subject to rust, so moisture and ventilation are important issues. Subject to denting. Lightweight; subject to damage from strong winds or heavy snow loads.
Permanence	If well constructed, long enough life span to be considered permanent.	Relatively short life span (5 to 8 years).
Care and maintenance required	Regular interior cleaning. Periodic repainting or restaining. Regular removal of leaves, twigs, and pine needles. Ventilation.	Regular interior cleaning. Periodic washing of exterior and waxing with good paste wax to help preserve finish. Touch-up painting of any scratches to prevent rust. Periodic tightening of screws and adjustment of doors. Regular removal of leaves, twigs, and pine needles. Removal of snow and ice from roof. Ventilation for heat and moisture.

A Comparison of Project Kits

Metal Sheds	Manufacturers of metal sheds offer the most complete prefabricated kits. Few tools are needed, and the basic skills required are patience and the ability to follow the instructions provided.		
	Package Includes	**Other Materials Needed**	**Comments**
Metal Shed Kit	Instructions. All structural parts and hardware.	Anchors. Flooring, if desired.	Probably the simplest type to build since you don't have to measure or cut materials, but the most limited in terms of design and customizing possibilities.

Wood Sheds	Kits for wood sheds can take many forms. Lumberyards and home centers commonly put together their own packages for wood sheds, using materials they have in stock. Parts included can vary greatly, but, in any case, assembly is likely to be a major construction project. Check what kits are available locally. Some of the approaches you might encounter are listed below.		
	Package Includes	**Other Materials Needed**	**Comments**
Precut Wood Shed Kits	Instructions. Precut wood framing. Precut sheathing. Hardware. Trim.	Paint. Incidental finish materials.	Few tools are required. Assembly is simplified; you don't have to determine, measure, or cut materials.
Partially Precut Wood Shed Kits	Instructions. Precut wood framing. Uncut sheathing. Hardware. Precut trim.	Finish materials. Possibly some metal framing components.	Precut pieces may be numbered to make assembly easier but you'll still need to do some measuring. Sheathing materials will need to be cut to fit.
Uncut Wood Shed Kits Kits listed here may be supplied with some, or none, of the wood required.	Instructions. Cardboard templates. Uncut framing and sheathing materials. Hardware.	Trim and finish materials.	Cardboard templates work like a dress pattern to guide measuring and cutting. Templates may be sold separately, with instructions and a lumber list, so you can choose your own materials. Measuring and cutting are simplified.
	Instructions. Metal connectors for framing. Paper templates.	Framing lumber. Sheathing materials. Carriage bolts and other hardware. Trim and finish materials.	This kit uses simple construction to create a very sturdy shed with a five-sided base. Templates simplify measuring and cutting. Connectors simplify assembly. Dimensions, styling, and materials can be varied to suit your needs.
	Instructions. Uncut framing and sheathing materials. Hardware.	Trim and finish materials.	This approach is the closest to building from scratch with traditional techniques, although you don't have to do a materials estimate.

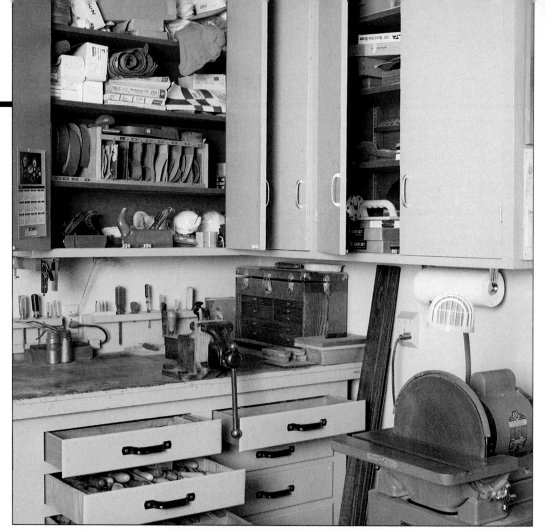

This small spare room makes maximum use of space. Wall-mounted cupboards supplement a freestanding tool and hardware cabinet, the top of which serves as a bench. The table saw, drill press, and bench are placed to take advantage of natural light.

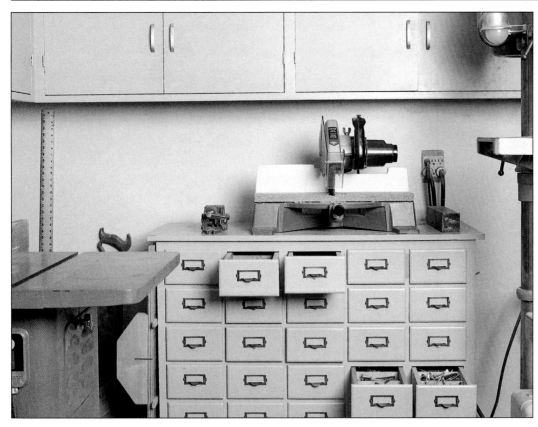

The opposite side of this workshop contains more wall cabinets and freestanding cabinet-benches. The power miter box, band saw, scroll saw, table saw, drill press, lathes, jointer, belt sander, and grinder all vie for the limited but well-organized space.

THE BASEMENT

The dream of every do-it-yourselfer is a complete workshop—a space in which to organize tools and work on projects that do not have to be cleared away whenever you are not working on them. The basement is the ideal location for such a shop.

Factors to Consider

The basement is ideal because it is easier to heat than a garage; humidity can be controlled better than in a shed or garage; noisy power tools are not as likely to disturb the family, as they are in a spare room or attic; and space need not be shared with cars and bikes. However, the basement may pose some of the same problems as the attic. Consider the following factors before you set up a workshop in your basement.

Headroom

You will need headroom, so examine all of the obstructions. There should be at least 80 inches of vertical clearance beneath any pipe, duct, or other obstacle protruding from the ceiling.

Floor Space

Is there enough space for a workshop? As with the attic there are codes for the use of basement space. A habitable room must usually measure at least 70 square feet. Check to see whether you have the minimum.

Structural Stability

Make sure that the basement is structurally stable. Examine the walls and floors. If there are cracks wider than ¼ inch in the walls, or if there are sunken spots in the floor, they will have to be repaired. You will need to seek professional help if any wood posts are rotten at the bottom, if flooring has separated from the top of the foundation, or if any joists are sagging. An architect, engineer, or foundation contractor can diagnose the problem and prescribe help.

Moisture

Is the basement dry? If there is a moisture problem, you must solve it before you install the workshop. This may well take months. Moisture comes from inside in the form of condensation and from outside in the form of leaks and seepage. Condensation occurs when cool surfaces collect moisture from warm air. If the basement is damp during hot weather, or if water is forming on the cold-water pipes, you are dealing with condensation. If the walls are damp and you aren't sure where the moisture is coming from, a little test will tell. Tape

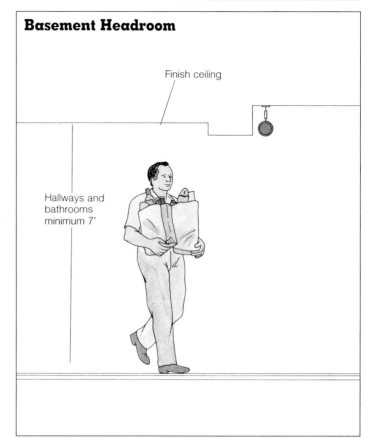

Basement Headroom

Finish ceiling

Hallways and bathrooms minimum 7'

This basement shop is narrow, but the machinery and workbenches make economical use of the existing space.

a piece of plastic sheeting to the wall and leave it in place for a few days. If water forms on the outer surface of the sheeting and the inner surface remains dry, the problem is condensation. If the inner surface is wet, seepage is the cause. Repeat the test in a couple of weeks to be sure.

To overcome these problems you may need professional advice. However, there are some things that you can do yourself. Adding more than one window, insulating pipes, and installing a dehumidifier can cure condensation. Keeping downspouts and gutters clear of debris and regrading around the house can often cure seepage. Inspect water, sewer, and air-conditioning pipes for leaks. If you repair all of these defects and moisture is still present, you will need to waterproof the interior walls and seal all cracks and joints with hydraulic cement. You may also need to install drainpipes and waterproofing to channel water away from the exterior walls. These are major repairs. Contact a soils engineer or a contractor specializing in drainage systems.

Power tools should always be used in a dry location. Damp floors greatly increase the risk of serious electrical shock, because damp concrete provides excellent conduction—from a defective tool right through you into the ground! Ground fault circuit interrupters should always be installed in basement workshops.

Safer Basement Access

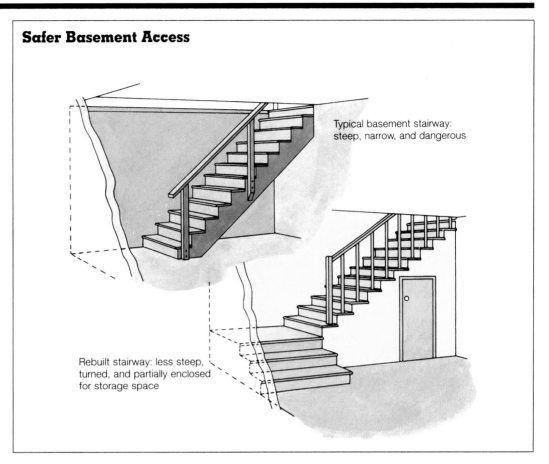

Typical basement stairway: steep, narrow, and dangerous

Rebuilt stairway: less steep, turned, and partially enclosed for storage space

Windows

Basements are not noted for their natural light. Such light as there is should illuminate work surfaces without causing glare. Enlarging a window well will increase light while dispelling that closed-in feeling.

Windows that open should be screened during the warmer months. If the windows do not have screens, you can make or buy simple units to pop in when you are using the shop. Cross-ventilation will reduce dampness (provided that the windows are closed before it rains) and will help to keep the whole house at an even temperature.

If there aren't any windows, a bulkhead with a screen works very well. Open the bulkhead door and lay across the top a homemade or purchased screen that overlaps the edges. You can easily push it out of the way if you need to make an emergency exit.

Stairs

Most codes do not specify that a basement have a direct exit the outside. As a rule, they only stipulate that an unfinished basement have secondary stairs. These are usually steep, narrow, and dangerous. The following are the typical code requirements for primary stairs.

7½-inch maximum riser height
9-inch minimum tread depth
32-inch minimum stair width
   between handrails
80-inch minimum headroom
30- to 33-inch handrail height
36-inch platform depth

If the existing stairs do not meet these specifications, build a new stairway or install one in a new location. Building a new exterior entry as primary access is a bigger project; you may need to consult a professional.

Outside Door

A door that allows access to the basement without going through the house is preferable if you will be carrying larger items in and out of the shop. Be sure that the stairway is not too steep or the steps too narrow. Use reflective tape on the overhead beam that protrudes at the base of the stairs.

Heating

It isn't usually difficult to heat a basement shop. If the house has a central heating system, chances are that the furnace is in the basement; it may give off enough heat for your needs. If it doesn't, tap into the nearest ducts and add new registers. If you have a hot-water system, it should be easy to extend some of the pipe into the shop area. Alternatively, you might opt to install electric baseboard or a small gas heater. (Remember that gas must be vented.)

Add some charm along with the heat by installing a wood-burning stove. Cut a flue opening and add chimney pipe as specified by the local code. Maintain minimum clearances between the pipe and any combustible materials.

Cooling the basement probably won't be a problem. Except in extremely hot climates, most underground spaces maintain a natural temperature of about 50° F. A fan will create cross-breezes if it gets too warm.

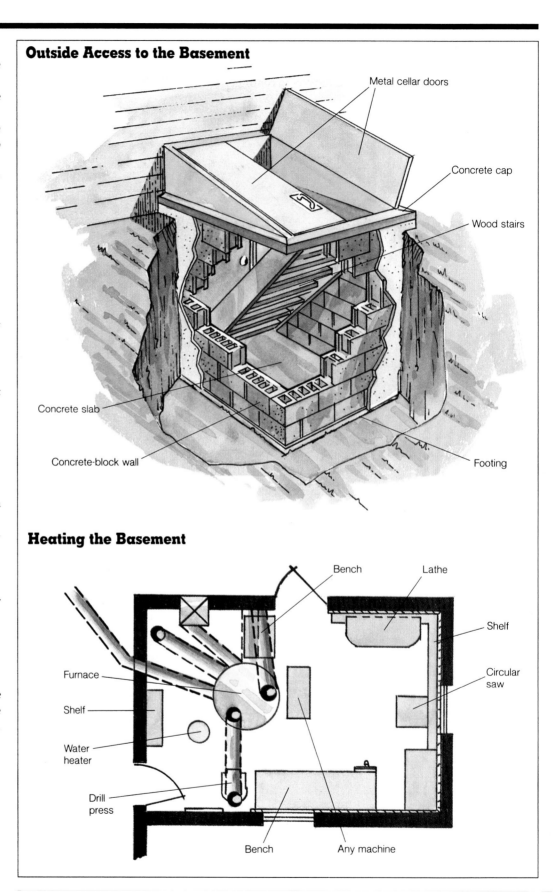

Outside Access to the Basement

Metal cellar doors
Concrete cap
Wood stairs
Footing
Concrete-block wall
Concrete slab

Heating the Basement

Bench
Lathe
Shelf
Circular saw
Furnace
Shelf
Water heater
Drill press
Bench
Any machine

Electrical Outlets

The importance of installing a GFCI has already been emphasized (see page 27).

Electrical outlets in the ceiling will provide power without a tangle of cords on the floor. Use them for stationary tools as well as power hand tools. A reel-in extension will keep the cords out of your way.

Obstacles

Obstructions in the basement can be dealt with in the same way as obstructions in the attic. Building around pipes, ducts, or other obstacles is usually easier than moving them.

Lighting

The traditional double-tube fluorescent lamp will provide bright, even lighting. A set of track lights can be installed to illuminate specific areas. A clamp light can be attached to a bar above the workbench. Walls should be painted in pale, bright colors. If painting isn't possible, cover the walls with light-colored acoustic material.

Comfort

A floor covering of wood or heavy vinyl should be laid down to ease the discomfort of standing on concrete. Spend some time and money on a comfortable floor; it's well worth it when you work long hours standing up.

Safety

You will need switches or circuit breakers to control each piece of equipment. Keep the lighting circuits separate from power circuits so that while the power is off the room may still be illuminated. Safety in the basement is important, because it is usually a shared area. A small child helping with the laundry might wander over to play with your interesting saws. Controls should be safety oriented. Lock away all switches. Install a master kill switch that controls everything except the lights. This switch should be at the shop entrance, out of your children's reach.

Cabinets for hazardous materials must lock, and they should be kept out of the reach of children. Some hazardous materials, such as solvents, require fire-resistant metal cabinets.

A fire extinguisher is a must in all shops. There should be one in the basement already if the furnace is located there. It's a good idea to have another one specifically for the shop. Hang it in plain sight, check it regularly, and show others how to use it.

Building a basement workshop from scratch is the ideal. In this one the electrical outlets are spaced evenly along the unfinished walls.

Basement Workshop Layout

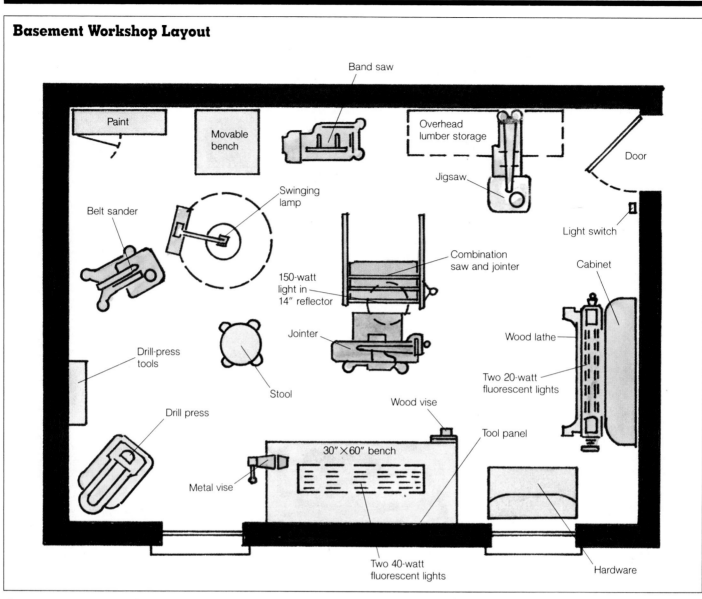

Band saw

Paint

Movable bench

Overhead lumber storage

Door

Jigsaw

Belt sander

Swinging lamp

Light switch

Combination saw and jointer

Cabinet

150-watt light in 14" reflector

Jointer

Wood lathe

Drill-press tools

Stool

Two 20-watt fluorescent lights

Wood vise

Tool panel

Drill press

30" X 60" bench

Metal vise

Hardware

Two 40-watt fluorescent lights

Organizing the Basement

A good basement workshop should have plenty of storage. Put dead space to work. The areas under the stairs, odd corners around the furnace, and shallow crawl spaces can all be utilized.

A well-organized shop has separate zones for workbenches, portable tools, and stationary equipment. A large cabinet or a pegboard hung from the ceiling could separate an electrical unit from a woodworking unit, for example. Be leery of hanging things from pipes unless you know that

they are sturdy and puncture-proof. A large rolling tool chest is a perfect addition to the basement shop. Rolling chests have between 2 and 20 drawers and come in many sizes. They cost from $100 to $400.

The Basement Workbench

Most of your work will be done on or around the workbench. The style and location of this bench should be determined as early as possible. Lighting, ventilation, access, and so forth will all fall into place after the workbench area is defined.

When completed this basement workshop will have a built-in dust collection system, a finishing room, a bathroom, and an office.

LARGE WORKSHOPS

The dream of every do-it-yourselfer is to have enough shop space to work on a number of projects simultaneously—to be able to spread out materials and still have room to work, and to have all of the necessary tools to do the job.

Large workshops may be created by converting a multicar garage, the ground floor of a barn, or a freestanding building, or by building an addition to the house.

If you are lucky enough to live in a rural area, a converted barn makes an ideal home workshop.

THE MULTIPURPOSE WORKSHOP

In a large space one can enjoy the luxury of a multipurpose shop. Such a shop might include areas for woodworking, metal work, auto repair, electronics, and other specialities.

The multipurpose shop tends to be more flexible than the single-purpose shop, because of the varied nature of the projects. It's a good idea to leave a large open space in this type of workshop. On one weekend the car may be in for repair, and on the next the boat may be in for painting. Casters might also be fixed to stationary machines, so that they can be rolled into the work area when needed. The multipurpose shop is ideal for people of varied interests, especially for the all-around do-it-yourselfer.

A Separate Office

The dream shop may also include an office with files, shelves, a desk, a drafting table, and a computer terminal. A closed, dust-free office provides a clean environment for the development and storage of plans. There is space for reference books on every subject from woodworking to plumbing. Even computers may become a common tool in the home shop. However, sensitive computers are damaged by wood dust; the shop computer will be protected in this office.

If the dream shop contains a computer, plans for a craft project may soon be ordered through the keyboard. They will be printed out modified to fit your particular specifications. These might include not only the style and complexity of the piece to be built, but also the skill level of the worker and the tools available. Plans would include complete drawings, bills of materials, directions, special machining instructions, and price. Plans ordered through the keyboard could be changed through the keyboard. One entry, and all of the dimensions, the bill of materials, and the price list would instantly reflect the new specifications.

Multipurpose Workshop

Cabinets

Spray booth

Grinder

Bench

Metalworking Shop

Wood rack

Metal bench

Drill press

Sander

Sink

Wood Shop

Drill press

Jigsaw

Office

Table saw

Desk

Wood lathe

Books

Planning board and bench

Fluorescent Lights Over Bench

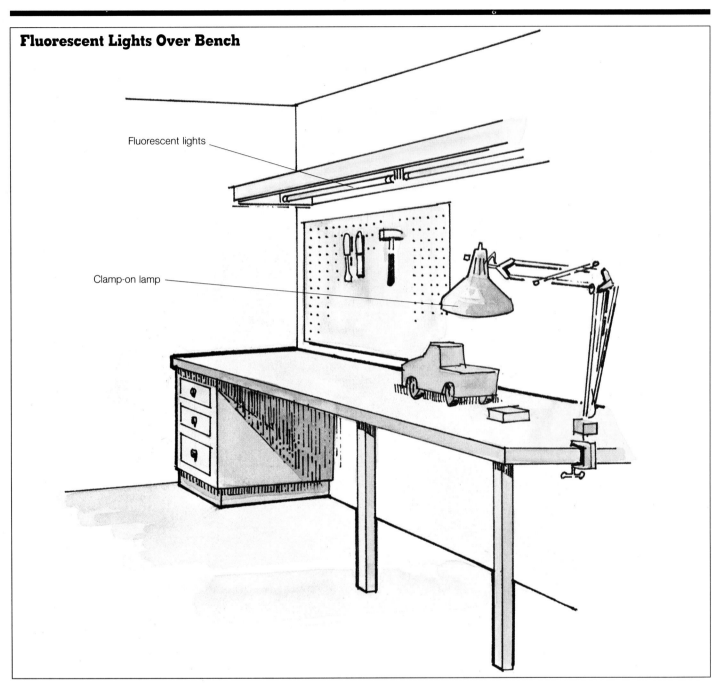

Fluorescent lights

Clamp-on lamp

Electrical Power

Be generous when it comes to power in the shop. Install a subpanel at the entrance that will amply supply your needs.

Space outlets no more than 48 inches apart around the perimeter of the room. There should be at least two or three on each wall. Install them high enough so that you can plug and unplug tools without bending over. Use grounded three-prong outlets rated for 20 amperes. Hang overhead outlets near each workbench area that is not near a wall. Each stationary tool should have its own designated outlet. No unplugging and replugging in your dream shop. Just go in, unlock the master switch, and get started.

Lighting

Plan to use as much natural light as possible, but don't forget to install full nighttime lighting as well. A shop with a variety of options is best. Overhead, fluorescent fixtures are a popular choice. Install wire mesh over them to protect them from getting broken. Fluorescents are relatively inexpensive, so purchase enough to illuminate the whole shop. Install overhead light switches at each entrance on a separate circuit from the master switch. Shops with dark walls and ceilings will require more lighting than shops with white ceilings and light-colored walls. A new coat of light-colored paint might be cheaper than extra fixtures.

Install at least one bank of lights directly over a wall-mounted bench. The lights should be placed close to the wall, so that you won't cast a shadow over your work. Install gooseneck lamps in areas that need special illumination, such as the workbench or the table on the band saw. Have several clamp-on lights that can be moved around the shop for special projects.

Heating

When it comes to heating the workshop, think safety first. Shops are dusty and full of combustibles. *Avoid open flames.* It is seldom necessary to heat the shop above 60° F when you are working. You may want the office to be slightly warmer. Insulation and weather stripping conserve heat and save fuel.

Exposure to the Sun

When you think about heating (or cooling), don't forget the sun. Allow the shop to soak up as much passive heat as possible by exposing the roof, windows, and skylights to the sunlight. Sunshine coming through glass will heat up a concrete floor, and the machinery of the shop will radiate heat as the shop cools. Leafy trees overshadowing the shop will cool it in summer. Trees that shed their leaves in winter will let the sun in.

Heat From the House

If the shop is attached to the house, consider extending the existing heating system into the new space. Most systems are built to accommodate at least a two-room expansion. Extending hot-air duct work is easiest. The duct may be shut off when not in use, and it takes very little maintenance.

Furnaces may be installed in an exterior wall to send heat directly into the shop space. Use ducts to channel heated air to the corners of the shop.

Wood-Burning Stoves

A stove is handy in that it can burn up shop scraps and provide heat at the same time. However, it will take up valuable floor space, for it needs a barrier area around it. You must keep it impeccably clean; shop dust on the top surface of the stove may smolder and ignite. Some dealers will install a new stove for you, otherwise a local independent contractor can do the job. Installation can

Wood-Burning Stove

An airtight stove is very efficient. Installation must conform to local fire safety code.

take anywhere from a few hours to a couple of days. You can install a stove yourself but you must comply with all local code requirements. Safety is the primary consideration and local codes require that wood-burning stoves be positioned at specific distances from walls and other surfaces that might combust from the intense heat stoves throw out. If you consider a wood-burning stove, ask the local building inspector for further information.

Electric Heaters

Electric baseboard heaters and radiant heaters are relatively inexpensive to purchase and install, but they usually cost more to operate than other units. Because it is almost maintenance free and provides quick heat, electricity is frequently chosen for shops that are heated only occasionally. If you install baseboard units, be sure to locate them where they can be kept clean and free of floor dust.

Spray-Painting Booth

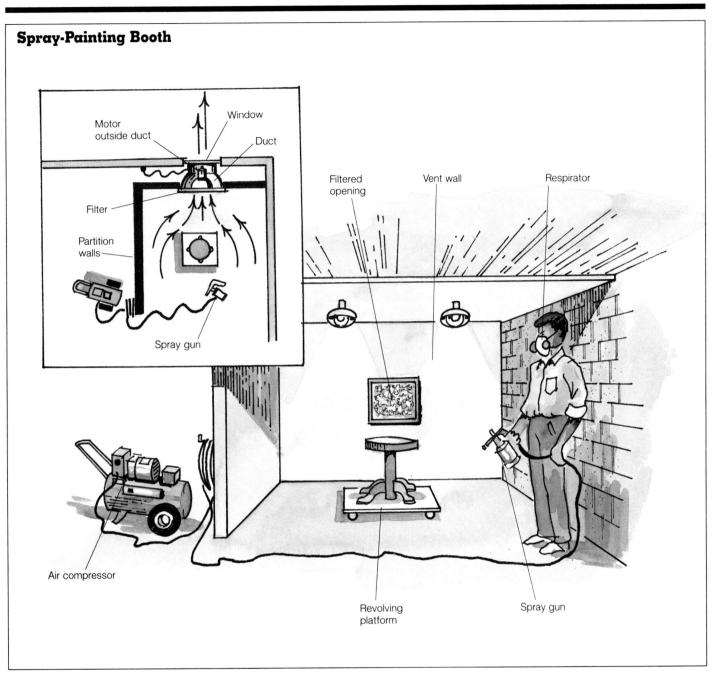

Motor outside duct

Window

Duct

Filter

Partition walls

Spray gun

Air compressor

Filtered opening

Vent wall

Respirator

Revolving platform

Spray gun

Air Compressor

Pneumatic tools—sanders, air wrenches, cutters, and drills— are a useful addition to your dream shop. They require an air compressor, which can also be used for spray cleaning and painting. Air is compressed into a holding tank and piped to all corners of the shop. Each tool is attached to an air line with a quick-connect coupling.

Spray Booth or Painting Area

A separate room for painting and finishing is another possibility for this shop. Ventilation to such an area is of paramount importance (see page 86). A vented booth for spraying varnishes and lacquers on completed projects can be located in the larger area, which offers more possibilities for adequate ventilation.

Dividing the Space in a Multipurpose Shop

In this dream shop you can indulge yourself with every tool imaginable. You can also include speciality areas, such as a photography studio or a dark-room. Design the shop care-fully to use the work space to its best advantage. Make a floor plan as described in the first chapter. Pushing around little cutouts instead of heavy ma-chinery will save you a lot of backache.

A Portable Workbench

The location of the workbench is all-important. In the multi-purpose shop consider having a portable workbench for hand-tool work as well as a stationary workbench.

The Metal Shop

A large shop can accommodate a separate area for metalwork-ing. Equipment might include a 6-inch lathe, a metal-cutting band saw, a power hacksaw, a milling machine, and an arc welder. As a precaution the arc welder should be near one of the doors, so that the fire hazard is lessened. Metalworking needs a separate workbench, because the oil associated with metal parts can damage any woodworking projects. The tools for this skill will be stored at hand.

Oil and oil-soaked rags must be stored safely and disposed of properly. See the safety rules on page 32 for further information.

This large shop combines metalworking and woodworking facilities.

Metal Shop

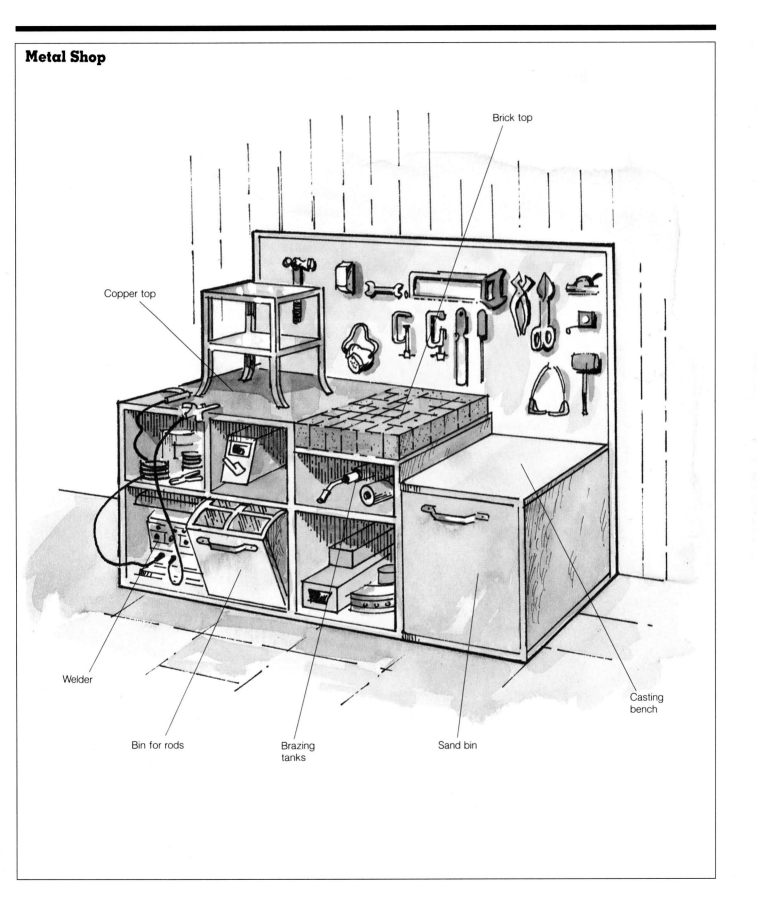

Brick top

Copper top

Welder

Bin for rods

Brazing tanks

Sand bin

Casting bench

Storage and Security

In the dream shop a mobile hardware cabinet can be moved around to meet various needs. The inside can be partitioned off to accept caddies and parts bins for nails, screws, and all sorts of fasteners. The top can be used as a small mobile work surface. If the cabinet is the same height as the table saw, planer, or jointer, it can be used as a temporary out-feed table.

The work that is done in the dream shop may require large quantities of supplies. In a barn or a three-car garage, there is often ample storage overhead. If you store lumber there, plan for proper ventilation in this area so that the wood will season properly.

If you want to be in this dream shop, so will other members of the family. Little ones need supervision; install locks and safety devices on all machinery. Now that you have a major investment in tools, you must guard against loss. Photograph the tools in the shop to keep an accurate inventory, and be sure that you have adequate insurance. Door openers with security options, infrared detection sensors at doors and windows, and a digital lock offer extra protection.

Ventilation

A fan will keep air moving away from a sanding operation, but it will just rearrange sawdust all over the shop if you don't exhaust the air outside or filter it. For this reason the fan should be set in a window or over an exterior door. If the shop has an open ceiling, consider an attic fan or a gable fan. These will exhaust air out and bring fresh air in below.

The powerful motor, filter, and fan assembly of a spray booth will filter airborne particles and exhaust fumes to the outside. If the workshop includes a spray booth, you must take the areas surrounding it into account. If you are inside the house proper, other rooms will be affected by the use of spraying devices. The exhaust and the noise of the fan should be channeled to minimize these effects.

Using Fans

Although it is relatively easy to exhaust air outside the shop to control dust and to provide fresh air, many shops, especially in cold climates, can't afford to throw heated air outside. Fresh air replacing exhausted air must be heated to room temperature, and this keeps the furnace on and wastes energy. A squirrel cage fan and a filter from a hot-air furnace can be adapted to resolve this problem at a fraction of the cost of a complete dust collection system. Squirrel cage fans are designed to move air throughout a house efficiently and quietly and are ideally adapted to a homemade system. They can be used in either of two ways. In the first, the motor and fan are enclosed in a box, on several sides of which the incoming air is drawn through furnace filters. In the second, dust-laden air is blown into a polyester felt bag, which filters out dust just like a vacuum cleaner.

Collecting Sawdust

Many manufacturers attach bags to sanders and other tools that cloud the shop with fine dust. These filter bags, when cleaned regularly, greatly reduce dust dispersal into the air. Consider sanding outside if the weather permits, especially if the tool has no filter bag.

You need space if your hobby is working on cars. This roomy auto shop is well organized and neatly maintained.

This dust removal system is housed in a closet on the outside of the shop. PVC pipe and flex hoses connect to the machinery inside the shop.

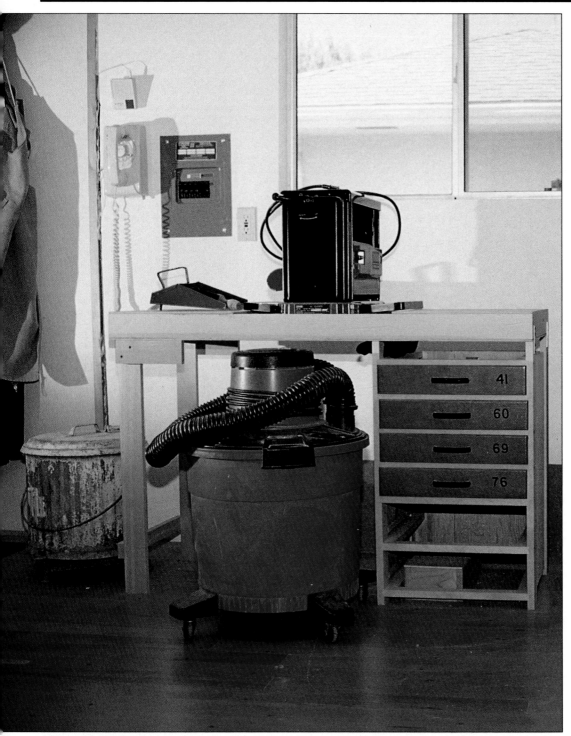

Paper Dust Masks

Even with the best ventilation system, you are bound to breathe in some shop dust. Keep a box of disposable paper dust masks on hand. These masks are not effective in screening out fumes, but they do a good job of filtering out dust. Make it a habit to wear one whenever you are sanding, routing, or cutting any material. Putting on a dust mask can quickly become an easy habit that will make you much more comfortable in the shop.

Shop Vacuums

A shop vac is an excellent investment; it keeps the machines clean as well as the floor. Set it up in a central location and it becomes a dust collector system while you are cutting or sanding. Many machines come with vacuum attachments; homemade attachments are easy to build with scrap materials and PVC drainpipe. Make one for each piece of equipment. The shop vac can easily be rolled to the spot and attached to any machine.

Built-in Shop Vacuums

Large shops may be fitted with dust removal systems built much like a central vacuum system for a house, although the motors and the pipe diameters tend to be larger. The system may be installed along the walls or overhead, depending on the shop layout. PVC drainpipe or metal pipe is used for the central system, and the

A portable shop vacuum is excellent for general shop cleanup and it can also be rolled to a specific machine to serve as a dust collecter.

Built-in Shop Vacuum System

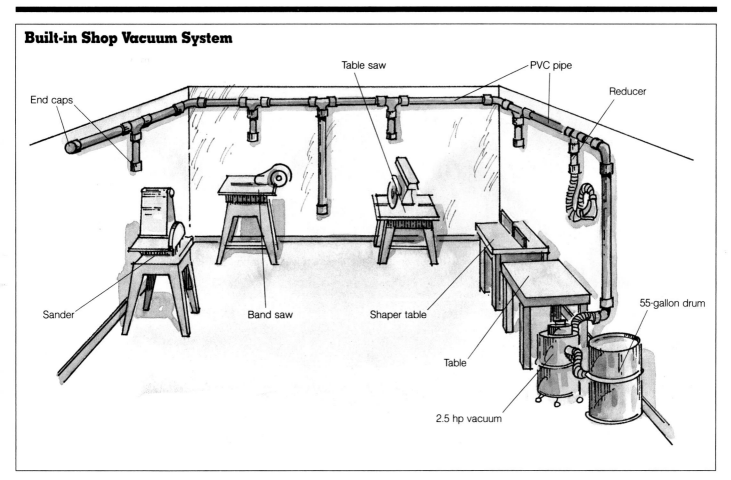

End caps · Table saw · PVC pipe · Reducer · Sander · Band saw · Shaper table · Table · 55-gallon drum · 2.5 hp vacuum

machines are connected with a short section of flex hose. (The flex hose is usually in short sections because it costs much more than rigid pipe.)

Important: Systems constructed with PVC pipe should have provisions to reduce static electricity in the pipe. Because the pipe is nonconductive, the passage of dust particles against the plastic will build up a static charge. One solution is to epoxy a grounded wire inside the pipe.

Connections with sanitary tees and long sweep elbows are best. These connections sweep air and debris along a wider angle than standard elbows, keeping air flowing better and reducing pipe clogs.

The system illustrated uses 3-inch PVC drainpipe along the perimeter of the room. Air is drawn into a 55-gallon drum by means of a 1-horsepower (hp) induction motor. Induction motors are often used on woodworking equipment, and they run more slowly and quietly than the brush motors commonly found in shop vacs. Each machine is hooked to the collection system with a short section of flex pipe and a homemade air valve called a blast gate. The blast gates may be closed on machines that are not being used, increasing air volume on the gates that are open. If too many blast gates

are closed, the fan motor becomes starved for air and will labor. When the system is installed, a little experimentation will determine how many blast gates should be open at one time.

In this shop there is a built-in sanding bench by the radial arm saw. It doubles as a table for the saw and the shaper. It consists of an ordinary bench top with holes drilled in it and a dust manifold built in below. Dusty air is pulled down through the bench, channeled into the dust collection system, filtered, and returned to the shop. A system like this keeps the dust away from your face as you sand.

The Photo Studio

If you need to photograph your pieces, it's nice to have a studio right in the shop. Allow enough space for a tripod and camera and for several lights. A back wall of seamless background paper will help you to achieve professional results. You might do some small-craft work in this area when it is not being used for photography. If you put in many shelves and storage units, you can use the area for more than one purpose.

The Three-Car Garage

In this garage the first two bays were converted into a working area, and the last was converted into a finishing area and clean office space. Two of the original garage doors have been replaced with walls, leaving the center one for moving large projects in or out. Here are some of the special features of this multipurpose shop.

The Woodshop

This area was formerly a one-car bay. It has a central workbench surrounded by tool storage and floor-mounted machines. The bench is massive, but like the table saw, jointer, and band saw, it is mounted on retractable casters. These allow the unit to be easily moved; they can be raised to provide a stable base. Power is supplied from retractable overhead cords. Both the table saw and the jointer are served by one cord that drops behind the fence of the jointer, so that it doesn't interfere with cutting operations. A dust system is installed overhead; the flexible hoses to the machines are hung up when not in use.

Cabinets

Spanning the end wall is a set of cabinets. All but one are the same height as the table surface of the spindle shaper and the radial arm saw. This convenient feature allows the tops of the cabinets to be used as extended tables for the machines. This is especially useful when attachments such as a sanding drum or a dadohead are used with the radial arm saw. A small door at the left end of the counter may be opened to extend the board outside. This feature makes it possible to shape, sand, or cut a board of any length.

The top of one cabinet is lower than the rest. The power miter box is stored here. This convenient feature adjusts the height of the power miter box table to the height of the rest of the counters. The power miter box is not bolted down; it may be moved out of the way of the shaper or transported to a job site.

The cabinets with doors provide clean storage for hand-held power tools, spare blades, and machine parts. Old kitchen cupboards with bright new paint get a second lease on life in this shop. The doors keep out sawdust and provide lockable security for expensive

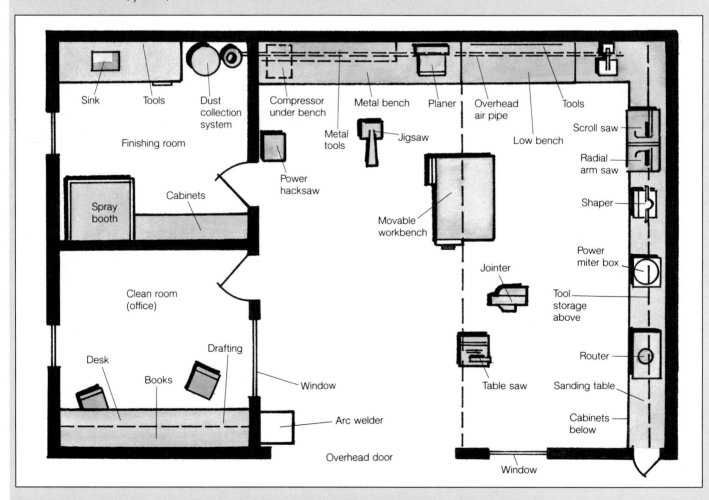

Sink — Tools — Dust collection system — Compressor under bench — Metal bench — Planer — Overhead air pipe — Tools — Scroll saw — Radial arm saw — Shaper — Finishing room — Metal tools — Jigsaw — Low bench — Power hacksaw — Cabinets — Spray booth — Movable workbench — Power miter box — Jointer — Tool storage above — Clean room (office) — Router — Drafting — Desk — Books — Window — Table saw — Sanding table — Arc welder — Cabinets below — Overhead door — Window

tools. The toe kick below the doors provides space for the feet of anyone who stands against the counter. It also makes sweeping the floor easy, since there are no table legs to sweep around.

Above the cabinets shallow shelves and tool cupboards span the full length of the wall around the window. Hand tools are hung two or three steps from the workbench. Higher and harder-to-reach shelves store hardware that is used only occasionally.

Rear Wall

The low bench in this area is used for seated work. A swivel stool on casters is comfortable and handy. Here is space for carving, soldering, or small-parts assembly. The bench is open underneath and constructed with braces to the back wall. This makes the floor easy to sweep, and there is nothing in the front to interfere with your legs. (A bench of this kind would be excellent for wheelchair access.) The wall behind the bench is used to store tools and small parts. The tools most often used are kept on caddies or hung low down to be within easy reach.

The thickness planer, complete with rolling stand and lumber rollers, is an occasional-use machine. In this shop it is stored along the rear wall. When it is needed it is rolled out into the work space and plugged into a receptacle. The casters are locked into place, and a flexible dust pipe hung overhead is attached to the planer hood to remove wood chips.

The rear wall in this area also has space for an interior dust control system consisting of a 55-gallon drum and a dust collector unit. Overhead, 4-inch dust removal ducts channel air into the collector from the table saw, jointer, planer, radial arm saw, and sanding table. Freestanding machines are made to be moved in this flexible shop, and the dust control system is designed to be flexible too. From an overhead distribution center, flex pipes drop to various locations, giving machines several floor spots in which to hook up. Each pipe is fitted with a blast gate, or sliding air valve, which may be closed when not in use and hung up out of the way. The blast gate on the sanding table is almost always left open to keep air moving through the dust removal system. This way, the fan motor is not overtaxed, and the air in the shop is continuously filtered when the system is turned on.

The Multiple-Use Space

The second bay of the shop has been converted into a space with many uses. A large project, such as a car or a boat, may be brought into the bay for repair. The center garage door is left intact so that big, bulky objects can be moved in and out.

The 4-foot workbench in the rear of this second area is designed for dirty use and for storing mechanic's tools. The countertop is easy-clean stainless steel and is fitted with a machinist's vice. The sink on the rear wall provides water for cleaning up. The rear wall is hung with pegboards and an assortment of hooks for storing tools. Air is piped overhead from a compressor in the finishing room; it is used to power pneumatic tools, clean dust and residue from tools and projects, and inflate tires. All the mechanic's tools are filed in a metal cabinet. Drawers can be taken out for on-the-job needs and returned to the cabinet when the job is done.

The Clean Room and the Finishing Room

The third bay of this shop layout is divided into two sections. The first is a clean room and the second is a finishing room. The partition between them has no window and is sealed tightly against dust.

Clean room This room functions as an office—a place to store books, drawings, a personal computer, and perhaps a sound system. It is also a place to plan projects, iron out mistakes, and find alternate solutions. It should have a comfortable overstuffed chair in the corner. It is a place for you to meet with clients if you plan to work for others. Computers are particularly sensitive to dust, so the office (including the ceiling) should be weather-stripped and sealed. If the room is cold, use a small electric heater or filter the incoming air from the furnace. A nice feature of the office is a windowed wall into the shop. This allows you to monitor another person at work, or to view a project as you contemplate the solution to a problem.

Finishing room This room is used for painting and finishing. It also contains a lockable, fire-retardant metal cabinet for storing chemicals. These include, beside finishing materials, products for automotive maintenance, cleaning, and gardening. (If the shop is allowed to cool below freezing, water-based products must not be stored here. It is dangerous to try to heat just the cabinet.) Along the back wall is a spray booth with an exterior exhaust fan. This explosion-proof unit filters air from the spray booth and doubles as an extra ventilator fan for the shop.

This freestanding workshop was built from scratch by the homeowner. The centerpiece of the shop is the table saw, around which other machines and benches have been arranged for easy access. For example, the homemade workbench has been strategically placed between the table saw and a long wall bench. Both benches and the table saw are but short steps away from the drill press, band saw, lathe, and jointer. All of the machines and benches have ample space around them for one to work comfortably. Double doors allow easy entry and exit for large projects. Several windows provide plenty of natural light during the day and overhead fluorescent lights permit night work. The guard for the table-saw blade is supported by a long curved arm that allows sufficient clearance for panels and other wide pieces of lumber. The wall space has been efficiently utilized for a lumber rack, tool cabinets, and bar-clamp storage. Electrical outlets are numerous and placed conveniently throughout the shop for machines and bench tools.

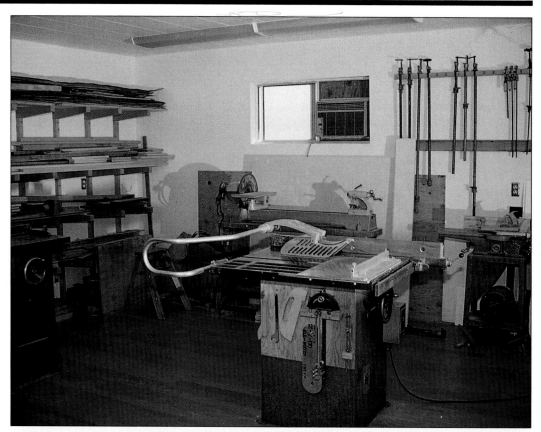

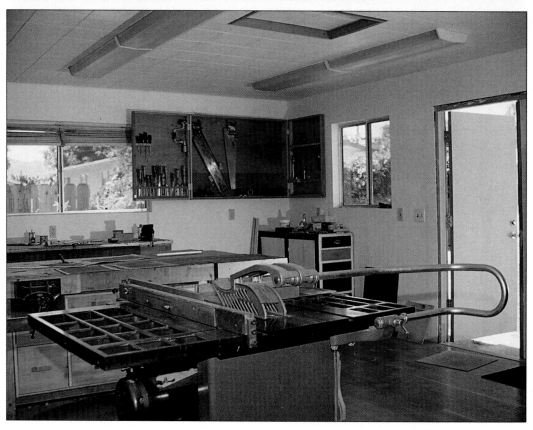

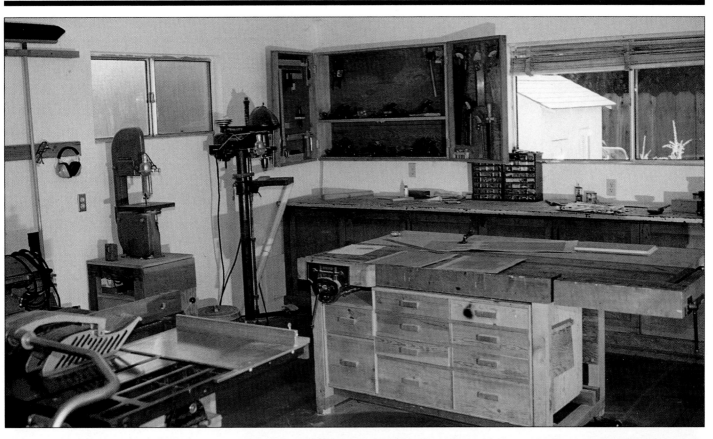

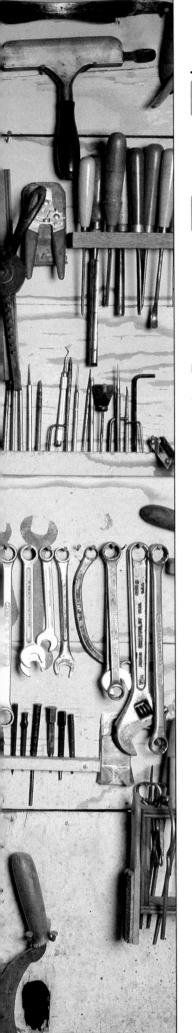

EQUIPMENT FOR THE WORKSHOP

A workshop isn't a workshop without equipment. The focus of the shop will determine the kind of equipment that goes into it. Because a tool is chosen for its function, you should understand clearly what you intend to do with it, how often you will use it, and the role it plays as part of a working unit.

Organize your tools so that you will always have the right one available for the job at hand.

BASIC EQUIPMENT

Many times space determines the choice of tools. Select tools carefully, especially if current space is restricted. Perhaps you don't have room for a heavy-duty power tool, but a hand-powered cousin might accomplish the same tasks and be small enough to be stored in a drawer.

Hand Tools

The tools are organized both by their function and by the approximate order in which many people purchase them. Listed first is a good all-around selection of hand tools that can be used to fix a sink, repair a door, paint a room, or even make a table. These tools are found in the professional's kit as well as in the novice's, because they are useful for such a great variety of tasks. Choose multipurpose tools whenever possible. For example, some chalk lines are housed in a case that is shaped like a plumb bob. Buy one of these and save the price of a bob.

Measuring Tools

Successful projects depend on accurate measurements. In choosing any measuring tool, note the quality of the craftsmanship. The measurement is only as good as the tool doing the measuring.

Steel Tape Measure

The retractable steel tape measure is a standard tool found on workbenches, clipped to belts, or deep in pockets. It has a hook on one end to secure it to the item that is being measured. A 50- or 100-foot tape may be necessary for measuring large distances, but a 12- or

16-foot tape is sufficient for most jobs. The best tapes are boldly marked in feet and cumulative inches. Often they are marked at 16-inch increments for setting or locating studs. Look for a model with a case that opens so that the tape can be replaced if damaged.

Bench Rule

This is like a school ruler except that, as the name indicates, it is kept on the workbench. Bench rules are calibrated down to $\frac{1}{16}$ inch, or even $\frac{1}{32}$ inch; they are favored by cabinetmakers. They are made of either steel or hardwood. The wood variety must be used on edge due to its thickness.

Folding Extension Rule

This used to be the basic measuring device in the workshop, but it is harder to find now than it once was. Made of hardwood, it remains rigid when unfolded, unlike the steel tape. A folding rule with an extension slide is good for measuring inside window framing.

Caliper

This tool consists of a pair of movable curved legs fastened together at one end. A caliper is handy when working on thickness dimensions for panels or molding.

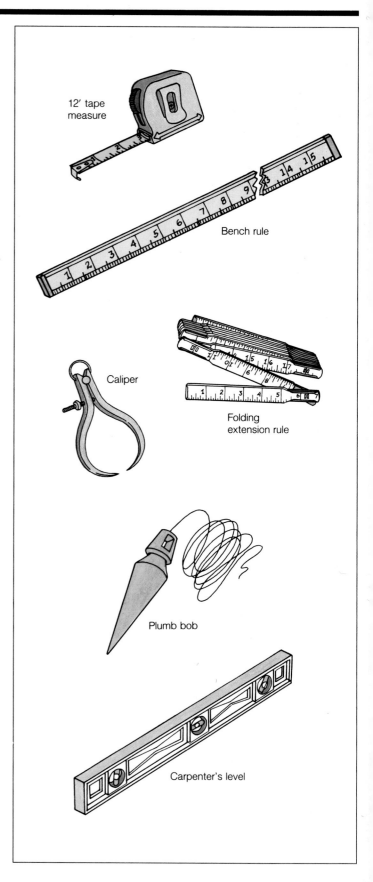

12' tape measure

Bench rule

Caliper

Folding extension rule

Plumb bob

Carpenter's level

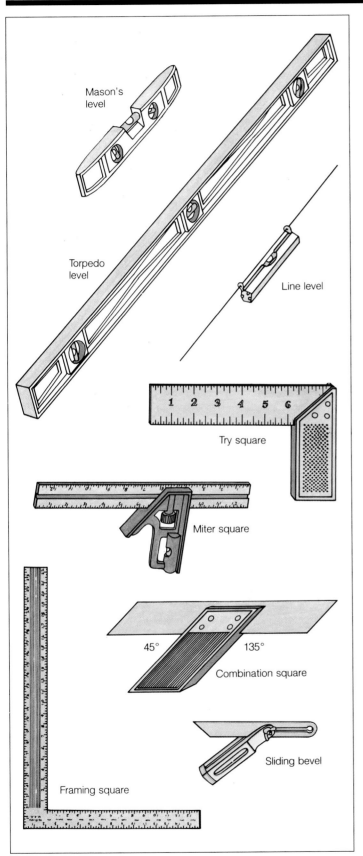

Mason's level

Torpedo level

Line level

Try square

Miter square

45°   135°

Combination square

Framing square

Sliding bevel

Plumb Bobs and Levels

A plumb bob is a lead weight hung at the end of a line. It is used to determine whether walls are vertical.

In all levels the principle is the same: A bubble in a glass vial of alcohol or ether moves to the center of the vial to indicate a true horizontal or vertical. A level must be handled and stored carefully to maintain its accuracy. Levels of high quality come in wood, metal, plastic, and combinations of these materials.

Carpenter's Level

This 2-foot level is often the elbow companion of the cabinet builder. A vial in the center checks the horizontal and a vial at either end checks the vertical.

Mason's Level

This level is up to 6 feet long. The additional length is needed to cover several blocks of masonry at once, so that it doesn't give a fast reading should one block be slightly out of true.

Line Level

Just a couple of inches long with hooks at each end, this little model can be hung on a piece of string. It is useful for giving approximations on long reaches, such as a building foundation layout.

Torpedo Level

Less than 1 foot long, this is a compromise between the carpenter's level and the line level. It is excellent for working in small, tight places. It too can be hung like a plumb bob by the holes at either end.

Try Square

This simple square consists of a 6- to 12-inch blade set at right angles to a hardwood or metal handle. It is used primarily to check square end cuts on boards and to mark cut lines. Its flat, broad edge also makes it handy for checking square corners in narrow places and for verifying that the blade on a table saw is perpendicular to the table.

Miter Square

A speciality tool, this square is used solely for marking 45-degree angles or bevels.

Sliding Bevel

This gadget adjusts to any angle; a wing nut holds it tightly at the desired setting. When you don't know the actual measurement of an angle in degrees, you can use this square to match it to the board you are going to cut. If you do know the exact measurement of an angle, you can place the sliding bevel on a protractor and preset it to the degree that is desired.

Combination Square

This workhorse is in and out of the carpenter's tool chest. It can quickly check 90- and 45-degree angles; it contains a small level; it can be used as a ruler or a marking gauge; and it includes a small scriber. If you can buy only one measuring tool besides the framing square, this is the one.

Framing Square

A framing square is used to check corners, but it has countless other uses ranging from laying out stair stringers to calculating rafter lengths. Usually one leg is 24 inches long, and the other 16 inches long.

Chalk Line

This tool consists of a piece of string wound inside a container of colored chalk. The chalk is replaceable. The chalk-coated string is stretched between two points and then pulled up and allowed to snap back. It quickly marks a long, straight line and eliminates the need for extensive penciling with a straight board. Most chalk lines can also double as a plumb bob.

Cutting Tools

Portable and stationary power saws have flooded the market in recent years with one highly advertised purpose—to save you energy. Sometimes they're worth using; other times its just as quick to grab a traditional saw and go to it. For every type of cut, there is a handsaw designed to do the job. You can select a good one if you understand what each kind of saw is used for.

Crosscut Saw

This is a general saw used for cutting across the grain. A good crosscut saw should have a highly flexible steel blade that gives a clear ring when tapped. This blade should be thinner along the back than along the cutting edge to lessen the chances that it will bind in the wood. It is tapered from the wider heel to the narrow toe. The teeth are beveled. The number of teeth per inch (TPI) is important; an 8-TPI blade is recommended for most jobs. It will provide an efficient but

slightly rough cut. Finer work, such as cutting moldings, may require the use of a 10-TPI blade. The number of teeth per inch is stamped on the blade near the handle.

Ripsaw

Cutting the board along the grain is called ripping. A ripsaw is normally 26 inches long, and the teeth are heavy and square faced rather than beveled. A ripsaw for all-around use may have 5½ teeth per inch. Like the crosscut saw, the ripsaw is tapered from the teeth to the back and from the heel to the toe.

Miter Box

Precision cutting at angles requires a miter box. This is a tool that guides a saw when cutting at an angle for a miter joint.

Backsaw

This is a short saw with a rigid back that prevents it from flexing and has 12 teeth per inch for smooth cutting. It is commonly used with a miter box to cut molding and trim at precise angles. Rabbets, grooves, and kerfs are often done with a backsaw.

Keyhole and Compass Saws

Curved cuts are done by hand with a keyhole saw or a compass saw. The compass saw has a long, flexible blade to negotiate curves easily. It is designed for working in tight corners or for cutting out the middle of a board. In the latter case, a hole is drilled in the wood and the compass saw is used to finish the job. Though the compass saw is sometimes called a keyhole saw, this term actually refers to a smaller saw used for

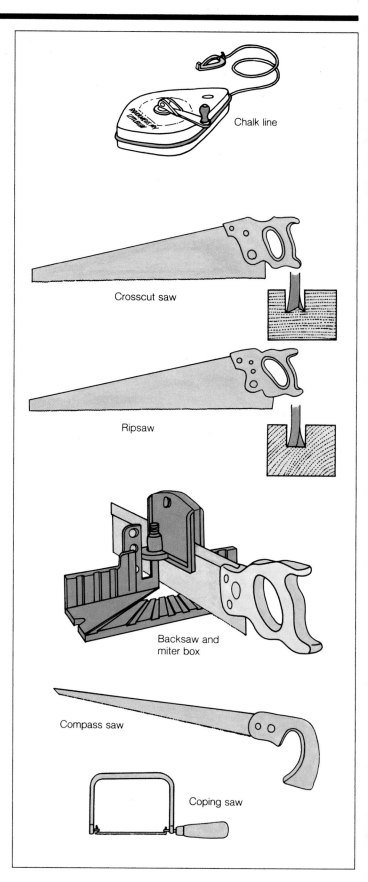

Chalk line

Crosscut saw

Ripsaw

Backsaw and miter box

Compass saw

Coping saw

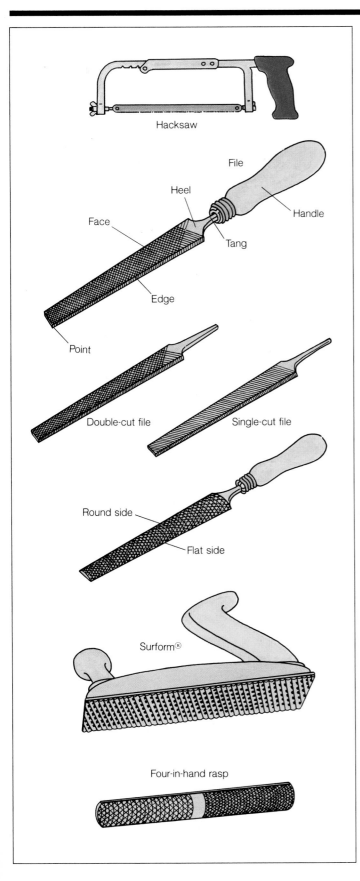

Hacksaw

File

Heel

Face

Handle

Tang

Edge

Point

Double-cut file

Single-cut file

Round side

Flat side

Surform®

Four-in-hand rasp

finer projects. It may be more logical nowadays to buy an attachment called a hole saw that can be attached to an electric drill. These come in diameters from ¾ inch to 4¼ inches.

Coping Saw

This saw has a thin blade with up to 20 teeth per inch. It is designed for cutting circles and patterns with tight curves. The blade can be removed from the saw, inserted into a hole drilled through a board, and reattached to the saw to make inside cuts. The blades are replaceable and can be rotated to allow clearance for the bow. The blades can also be reversed, so that the saw can cut on the pull stroke instead of the push stroke.

Hacksaw

Not a woodworking tool, the hacksaw is nevertheless essential to any shop. It is used to cut metal. Blades with 14 teeth per inch cut aluminum, brass, bronze, or steel. Blades with 24 teeth per inch cut copper tubing or iron. Get yourself a minihacksaw to use in the many places where the standard saw won't go—to cut nails under shingles, for example.

Surfacing Tools

In woodworking or finish carpentry, surfacing is the visible part of the job. It is also done during the building process, when each component is finely surfaced to fit. Surfacing tools include hand-held and power planes, jointers, files, rasps, Surforms®, sandpaper, and scrapers. They also include putty knives and wallboard knives; the latter are used to

smooth wall surfaces to prepare them for painting or papering.

Files and Rasps

There are more than three thousand kinds of files and rasps. Files are used on wood and metal. Rasps are used on wood. Files have ridges; rasps have individual triangular teeth. Rasps do rougher but much faster work than files. Files and rasps are from 4 to 14 inches long.

Single-cut files have parallel ridges running across the width of the blade. They are used for fine work. Double-cut files have ridges running at right angles to one another in a checkerboard pattern; they are used for coarse work. The four basic types of files are coarse, bastard, second cut, and smooth. Each type has progressively smaller spaces between the ridges, resulting in progressively smoother work.

Handles for files and rasps can be purchased separately. The tang, or pointed end, of the file is forced into the handle. Buy comfortable handles; it's safer and it gives you more control.

Surform®

Used for the rough shaping of wood, this tool is shaped like a plane, and looks like a cheese grater. It is easy to hold, and the interchangeable coarse or fine rasps screw into the base.

Planes

You should have a jack plane, a smoothing plane, and a block plane. All are available with wood or metal bodies, and all have similar cutting irons.

Jack Plane

This is used for working rough timber to size and for removing large amounts of wood from the straight board. A jack plane is about 14 inches long and 2 inches wide. Its soleplate bridges depressions and cuts only the high spots.

Smoothing Plane

This plane is used for finer work. Its 8- to 10-inch soleplate will produce a smooth, thin curl when you have reached the end of the planing stage.

Block Plane

This plane is smaller and more compact than the other planes; it can be held in one hand. It is excellent for smoothing corners, beveling, or removing a small amount of wood for a final finish.

Chisels and Gouges

These tools come in many shapes and styles; they are used for trimming and shaping. Chisels come with wood or plastic handles. For rough carpentry work plastic handles are preferable, because they are stronger. The end of the handle should have a steel cap for protection against taps from a mallet or hammer.

Butt Chisel

This chisel has a thick blade about 3 inches long and from ¼ inch to 1 inch wide. It is used for heavy work, such as trimming rough boards for a smooth fit or cutting out notches. Most carpenters keep a 1-inch butt chisel in their belt for rough trimming.

Bench Chisel

As the name indicates this is the workbench chisel. It is used by cabinetmakers for precision cutting. There are three types of bench chisels. The lightest of the chisels, the paring chisel is beveled 15 degrees for delicate work. The firmer chisel is a medium work tool, with the edge beveled 20 degrees. The framing chisel removes large amounts of wood with its 25-degree edge.

Gouges

Unlike chisels, gouges are used primarily for carving and for cabinetwork. Their blades are curved for cutting grooves and hollows.

Fastening Tools— Hammers

Any workshop, even a shop that consists of one kitchen drawer, needs two or three different hammer types. Hammers come in many weights and styles, each being appropriate for certain jobs. The weight is stamped in ounces on the hammerhead.

Curved-Claw Hammer

This is the basic hammer for every shop. A good general-purpose weight is 16 ounces. The curved claw enables you to remove small- to medium-sized nails with a rocking action that does minimum damage to the wood.

Ripping Hammer

Sometimes called a framing hammer, this heavier member of the family is used for construction carpentry. It has claws that can be used to pry

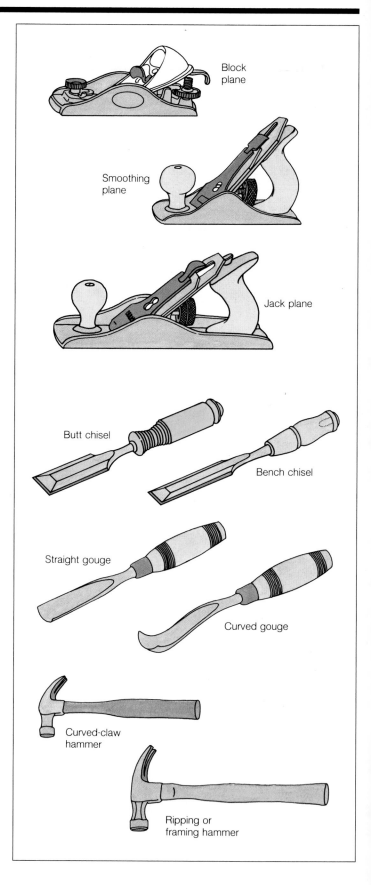

Block plane

Smoothing plane

Jack plane

Butt chisel

Bench chisel

Straight gouge

Curved gouge

Curved-claw hammer

Ripping or framing hammer

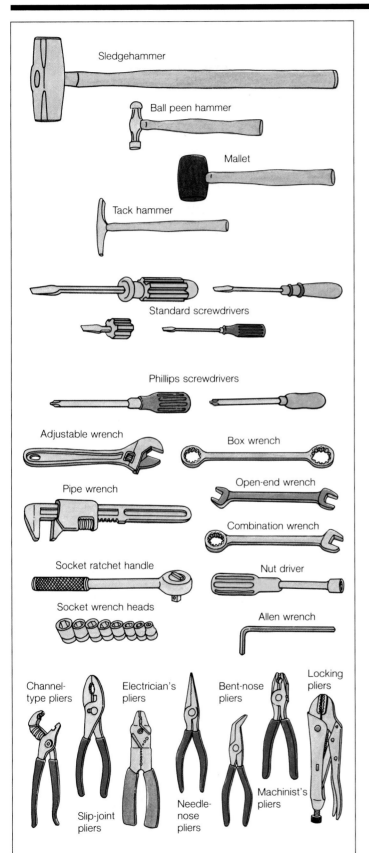

Sledgehammer

Ball peen hammer

Mallet

Tack hammer

Standard screwdrivers

Phillips screwdrivers

Adjustable wrench

Box wrench

Pipe wrench

Open-end wrench

Combination wrench

Socket ratchet handle

Nut driver

Socket wrench heads

Allen wrench

Channel-type pliers

Electrician's pliers

Bent-nose pliers

Locking pliers

Slip-joint pliers

Needle-nose pliers

Machinist's pliers

up boards, and to pull nails with a side-to-side motion. It weighs from 20 to 28 ounces.

Sledgehammer

Weighing up to 20 pounds, sledges are used to knock beams out of place, to take down walls, and to drive wedges.

Ball Peen Hammer

This hammer is used primarily in metalworking. Its head is flat on one end and round on the other. It is valuable in any shop, because the head is made of a specially hardened steel. For this reason, it can be used to break up concrete.

Mallet

A mallet is a hammer with a leather, rubber, or plastic head. If damage to the hammer is a consideration, use this tool. It will pack the wallop without chipping.

Tack Hammer

This small, fine tool has a magnetic head. Weighing 5 to 8 ounces, it enables you to drive brads, tacks, and nails without hitting your thumb. It is worth having one of these in the workshop.

Fastening Tools— Screwdrivers

Screws hold wood better than nails, so you will need a wide selection of long and short standard and Phillips screwdrivers. Make sure that you have several long-shank, straight-tipped ones for deeply recessed screws.

Wrenches and Pliers

No workshop can call itself complete without an assortment of wrenches. They are used for tightening or loosening nuts and bolts, turning lag screws, and working on pipes.

Adjustable Wrench

This is the backbone of the tool shelf and should always be close at hand. The standard adjustable wrench comes with 8- or 12-inch jaws. You might want to have two of these—one for holding and one for tightening.

Socket Wrench

This wrench is used with a selection of sockets that range from $\frac{3}{8}$ to 1 inch in diameter. Socket wrenches are also available in metric sizes.

Pipe Wrench

This is another standard for the home workshop, and again you need two of them. This wrench will loosen large nuts and bolts that are badly burred or that refuse to turn.

Other Wrenches

The box wrench, combination wrench, and open-end wrench all come in diameters ranging from ¼ inch to 2 inches. They have two openings of different sizes, one at each end. Allen wrenches are used for allen-head screws.

Pliers

There are several specialized kinds of pliers. A useful collection for the workshop might include: slip-joint, needle-nose, machinist's, channel-type, electrician's, and locking pliers.

Portable Power Tools

Power tools make the job go faster, and they can be easier to master than hand tools. On the negative side they are bulkier and more expensive. They offset their greater cost by their speed and accuracy, however.

There is a bewildering selection of power tools on the market. Each kind is available in a wide range of prices and qualities. Fortunately updated product guides are published in woodworking and mechanical magazines. Use these guides to aid you in your selection. Tools designed for the home shop are usually lighter than their industrial counterparts, less expensive, and easier to handle; with occasional use they will last for years. Frequent daily use may require the purchase of professional tools. These have larger motors and bearings, and a reputation for longevity.

Circular Saw

This is the biggest time-saver in a home workshop. A portable circular saw will do the job in a fraction of the time that a handsaw would take. Within the limitations of its blade diameter, it can be adjusted for either shallow or deep cutting. The base plate can be adjusted to cut bevels of any angle between 45 and 90 degrees. The circular saw has a multitude of blades for making different kinds of cuts or for cutting different materials from plywood to plastics.

The housing of a circular saw is made either of metal or of tough plastic. The handle is equipped with a trigger switch.

There is a spring-activated blade guard that slides up out of the way as the blade enters the material. In addition to the adjustable base plate, good saws have an adjustable rip fence that slides along the edge of the board when cutting wood.

The circular saw is classified by the size of the largest blade that it will accept. These sizes usually range from 6½ to 10 inches. Smaller saws are used for trim and flooring work. Professional construction carpenters use the larger models, but the 7¼-inch saw found in most home workshops will cut through a 2 by 4 when set at a 45-degree angle.

The higher the horsepower (hp), the more smoothly the saw runs, the faster it cuts under load, and the longer the motor will last. Choose a saw with the highest horsepower that you can afford.

The quality of the blade is as important as the quality of the saw itself. There are many different kinds of blades, each one designed for a specific job. Following are some basics.

Crosscut Blade

This blade has a series of evenly spaced, medium-sized teeth that are set, or bent, alternately to the left and right. They are sharpened on the inside, to provide a smooth cutting action across the grain.

Rip Blade

The teeth on this blade are also set alternately to the left and right, but unlike crosscut teeth, they are sharpened on the top, not on the inside. They are, in effect, a series of chisels that

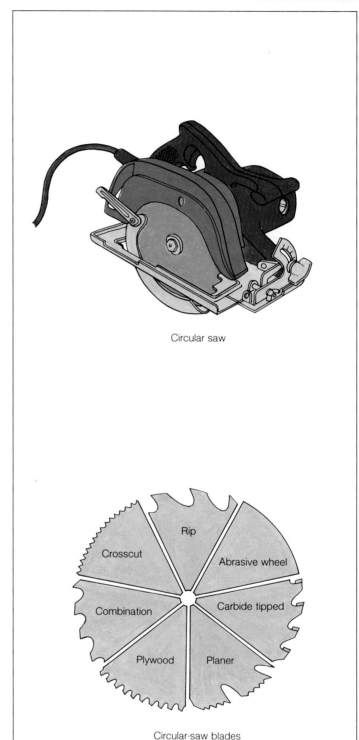

Circular saw

Circular-saw blades

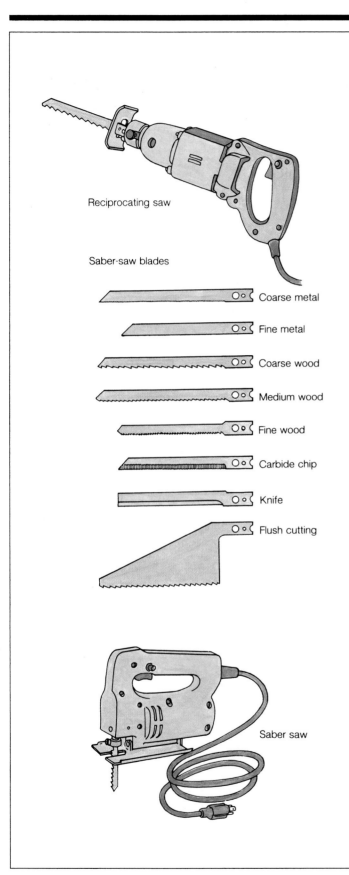

Reciprocating saw

Saber-saw blades

Coarse metal

Fine metal

Coarse wood

Medium wood

Fine wood

Carbide chip

Knife

Flush cutting

Saber saw

scoop out wood as the saw moves with the grain.

Combination Blade

The combination blade, which incorporates features of both the rip and the crosscut blades, is normally sold with new circular saws. It is the best choice for general shop and construction work, because it does both equally well.

Plywood Blade

With its many small teeth, this blade makes clean cuts through plywood. Crosscut and combination blades can also be used to cut plywood, but the larger teeth may produce splinters. Rip blades will really tear up plywood; they are a poor choice for the task.

Carbide-Tipped Blade

This is another general-purpose blade, but the long-lasting cutting edges are made from extrahard carbide steel. This blade is a good choice on construction sites, where large volumes of different materials are often cut.

Abrasive Wheel

This wheel has no teeth; it literally grinds its way through the material being cut. Some abrasive wheels are made for cutting masonry or fiberglass; others are made for cutting light metal. Don't try to cut something that the wheel is not specifically designed to cut. The blades are tough, but they are also brittle. Never twist the blade in a kerf with the saw running. It could shatter, with disastrous results for you and any bystanders.

Saber Saw

Also called a jigsaw, this is a valuable tool for any workshop. It cuts efficiently with a wide variety of blades, each of which is designed for a special task. Light enough to operate with one hand, the saber saw is also a good choice in tight places where a circular saw won't fit. Many beginners find that using it is like using a hand mixer or an electric drill.

Saber saws are rated at from $\frac{1}{6}$ to $\frac{1}{2}$ hp or more. Higher horsepower provides stronger sawing action and less wear on the motor. A $\frac{1}{2}$-hp model is suitable for the general workshop. A saber saw with higher horsepower is usually considered a commercial model. Select a two-speed or variable-speed saw, because different speeds are used to cut different materials.

A good saber saw will have a base plate that tilts from 90 to 45 degrees for bevel cuts. It will also have settings that move the blade in a slight orbit forward on the cutting stroke and back on the return stroke for rapid cuts and easy chip removal.

The rule of thumb for saber-saw blades is to match them to the material to be cut. For cutting hardwood, or for finish cuts on any wood, use a blade with 14 or more teeth per inch. For rough cuts on plywood or softwood, use a blade with fewer and larger teeth. (Fewer teeth per inch result in a coarser cut.) For cutting metal, choose a blade made from hardened steel, which will not overheat and snap.

Reciprocating Saw

The saber saw has a big brother that is often found on construction sites. The reciprocating saw is used by carpenters to cut large beams or posts and by plumbers to cut holes for pipes. If remodeling is on the horizon, this tool should be on your wish list. You can use it to cut right through wallboard. Choose a variable-speed model if you are planning to cut metal as well. It will operate at a speed slow enough to keep the blade from overheating and breaking.

The better the saw, the greater variety of blades it will take. The blades for a reciprocating saw are from 2½ to 18 inches long and can be mounted with the teeth facing either backward or forward. A standard set might contain 6-inch smooth-cutting, 6-inch flush-cutting, 5-inch metal-cutting, and 4½-inch sheet metal–cutting blades.

Miter Saw

If you plan to do a lot of jointing with miters, think about buying this power tool. It looks like a circular saw mounted on a hinge at the back. The motor pivots up and down and is adjustable left and right of center. The 14-inch (or less) blade is brought down onto the work, which is held against a fence. It will produce a very smooth, accurate miter cut.

Electric Drill

If you have only a tiny workshop, have very little money for tools, and want the most for the money, buy a power drill first. With the right accessories this simple tool can be used as a grinder, buffer, drill press, sander, chisel, screwdriver, wrench, and paint mixer. It can also be used, of course, to drill holes in almost any material.

Electric drills commonly come in ¼-, ⅜-, and ½-inch sizes. These sizes refer to the diameter of the largest bit shank that the drill can hold. Larger and more powerful drills are designed for commercial use.

The ⅜-inch drill with reverse gears and variable speed is generally a good choice for the home workshop. The variable speed allows you to tackle a variety of jobs without overheating the motor. The slow speed also allows you to use the drill as a wallboard screw gun. A reverse switch makes it possible to remove screws as well.

Buy quality. The longer the cord, the better the drill. Some models come with the chuck key attached to the cord.

Drill Press Stand

A drill can be used to create a whole workshop center. Choose a model that comes with plenty of attachments. Then add a drill press stand. (This is worth buying anyway if you plan to do a lot of precision drilling.) Mount the drill on the stand and add a grinding wheel; this gives you a grinder. Add a sanding drum; this gives you a sander. You can also attach a wire brush, a buffing wheel, and so forth. The stand is light and portable.

Router

A power router is an invaluable tool to own. It makes fancy edges on tables or cabinets, cuts dovetails in minutes, professionally trims plastic laminates

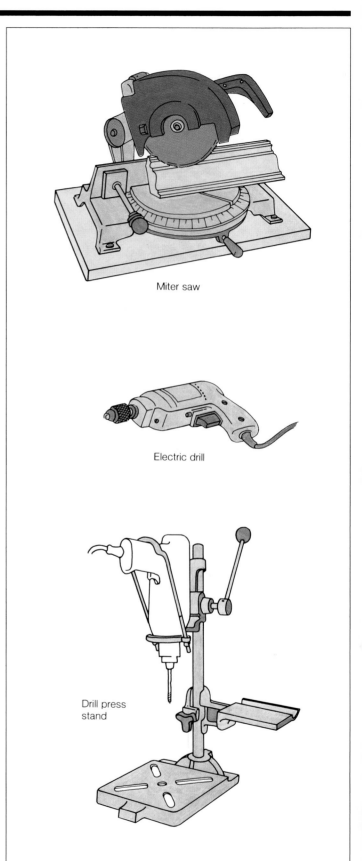

Miter saw

Electric drill

Drill press stand

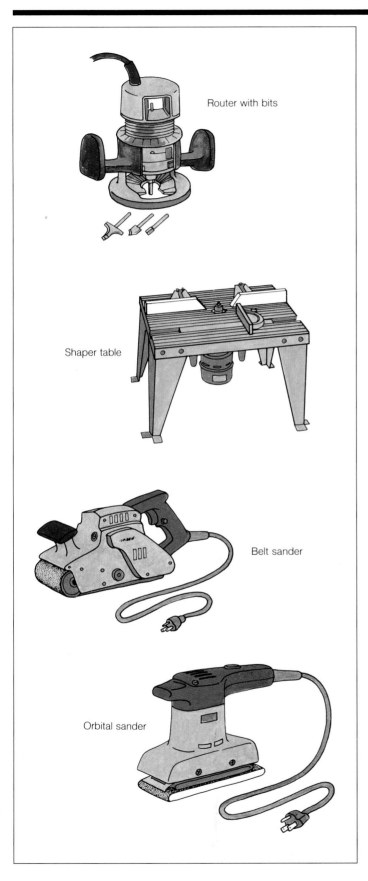

Router with bits

Shaper table

Belt sander

Orbital sander

used on countertops, and makes molding. When you have mastered this machine and have used it for a short time, you will wonder how you ever lived without it.

The router has a motor that drives a shaper bit at tremendous speeds—up to 27,000 revolutions per minute (rpm), compared to the 2,200 rpm for the average drill. This motor can be raised or lowered to adjust the cutting depth of the bit. A scale on the housing is used to set the depth, which can be as fine as $1/1000$ inch. Motors range from $1/2$ to 3 hp. The smaller the motor, the harder it must work to do the job and the faster it wears out.

There is an impressive selection of bits on the market. They are designed to make either grooves or edges, and they will cut all sorts of shapes in an enormous range of applications. Bits are made of high-speed steel or of the much harder tungsten carbide. If you are doing any work on plastic laminates, carbide bits are a wise choice. They last longer and they produce mirror finish cuts. Since there are so many varieties of bits, and since they are expensive, it is a good idea to buy a basic selection kit first. Then you can buy other bits as you need them.

Shaper Table

If you are doing a lot of cabinetwork or decorative work, this table could be a very wise investment. The router is fixed underneath it, and the wood is guided along a fence fixed to the top. Pick a sturdy model, or make one of your own. Many shaper tables have a grooved top to prevent sawdust from building up under the workpiece.

Sanding

All finish woodworking involves sanding. Traditionalists will spend hours hand-sanding for fine results. Power sanders do the job very well and considerably faster. An orbital sander makes 9,000 strokes a minute; hand-sanding as hard as you can, you might make 300 strokes a minute. If your workshop will be turning out any furniture, buy a belt sander, an orbital sander, or a random-orbit sander.

Belt Sander

The size of the abrasive belt determines the size of the sander. Belts range from 2 to $4\frac{1}{2}$ inches wide and from 21 to 27 inches long. The bigger the sander, the faster it does the job. An all-purpose, heavy-duty sander takes a 3-inch by 24-inch belt. This size is suitable for ordinary workshop purposes.

Sander belts range from 50 grit for very coarse sanding down to 220 grit for very fine sanding. This information is stamped inside the belt. An arrow is also stamped inside that indicates which way the belt must run. There is a corresponding arrow on the machine. Make sure to install the belt so that both arrows are pointing in the same direction.

Orbital Sander

Also called the finish sander, this little tool works more slowly than a belt sander but produces finer results. The orbital sander rotates in a tight circle, each stroke moving only $\frac{3}{16}$ to $\frac{1}{4}$ inch. Because it is sanding in all directions, you don't have to follow the grain.

The paper is held by clamps at each end. Be sure to fit it tightly over the sanding pad.

Random-Orbit Sander

This sander, originally used for auto body work, has been adapted to woodworking as well. It uses replaceable stick-on sandpaper disks and produces fine, high-speed finishes. It is slightly faster than an orbital sander, but it creates more airborne dust. The self-stick disks are more expensive than the disks used on orbital sanders.

Bench Grinder

It is essential that you keep all your tools sharp and clean. That is the function of the bench grinder. It is fairly expensive, but it will repay the investment by providing you with years of good service from your other tools. Shop around for the best model at the best price. Sometimes you can get a good deal at a flea market or a garage sale.

The typical bench grinder has two abrasive wheels, or stones, one medium coarse and one medium fine. A steel wire brush for cleaning and buffing is often interchanged with one wheel. A good bench grinder should also have adjustable plastic guards over each wheel and a small adjustable bench rest below each wheel. Set the bench rest to the proper angle before you begin sharpening any tool.

Stationary Power Tools

A woodworker's dream shop will include a table saw, a radial arm saw, and a power miter box for cutting square, rectangular, and mitered stock. It will have planers and jointers for surfacing and edging lumber. It will have a band saw and a scroll saw for cutting curved lines. It will have a shaper and routers in vertical or horizontal tables. Even a model shop will probably include at least one drill press for drilling, pressing, and sanding. A dream shop may also include multiuse machines.

Table Saw

The most important tool in the dream shop is located so that it need never be moved. It stands near a workbench of the same height as the saw; this makes it possible to cut long boards. A set of roller stands can be used with the table saw as well as the planer or jointer when there are many boards to be cut, but the ideal would be to have an out-feed table positioned behind the table saw. Wood can slide easily over such a table if it has a smooth, laminated surface. A table with a shelf below could be used to store jigs and push sticks.

A table saw consists of a motor and a circular saw mounted beneath an aluminum, steel, laminated plywood, or cast-iron table. The lighter models may have to be bolted to the shop floor for stability. The additional weight of cast iron stabilizes vibration and increases accuracy, making it the first choice of most woodworkers.

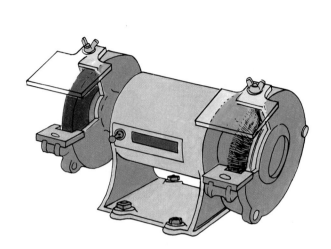

Bench grinder

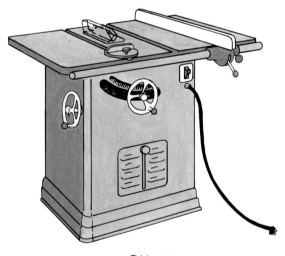

Table saw

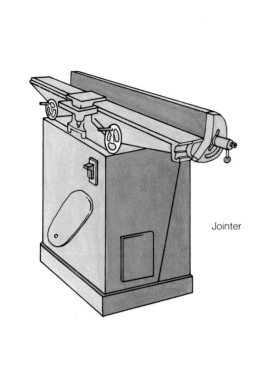

Jointer

Planer

The size of the table saw is determined by the size of the largest blade it will accept. These blades range from 6½ to 12 inches in diameter. The 9- or 10-inch saw is very popular with do-it-yourselfers and cabinetmakers. A professional contractor may prefer a 12-inch table saw.

The saw blade may be adjusted up and down and slanted to angles of from 45 to 90 degrees. Wood is pushed through the saw against a fence (for ripping) or guided past the blade by an adjustable miter gauge (for crosscutting). These two devices enable you to make consistently accurate cuts with the table saw. The fence is a flat bar, usually with a scale on it, that remains parallel to the saw blade. It can be locked in place at any distance from the blade to control the width of ripping operations. The miter gauge moves in a groove parallel to the saw blade, but the end that rests against the wood is adjustable. It is normally kept at 90 degrees to provide a square cut when crosscutting wood to length, but it can be adjusted to any angle up to 45 degrees. It is a common first purchase for most handicrafters, because it does a nice, accurate job of cutting rectangular parts.

The table saw will rip and crosscut most parts to size for bookcases, shelves, boxes, drawers, and so forth. It will also cut miters and bevels for picture frames and the like, because both the blade and the miter gauge are adjustable as described above. With a few extra jigs and fixtures, it will cut dado joints, box joints, and even curved molding. The great majority of woodworking projects, even something as exotic as a leg for a Queen Anne chair, are constructed out of flat and square posts. The great versatility of the table saw makes it the mainstay power tool of the shop. It is wise to position the table saw in a central location, close to the workbench and the jointer.

Jointer

In your dream shop there is a jointer parked close to the table saw. The jointer is often called a jointer-planer, because it joints the edges of boards and also planes surfaces up to the width of the jointer bed. Don't confuse it with the thickness planer described in the next section. Both operate by passing wood over or under a cylindrical cutter head.

The jointer has two tables with a cutter head in between. The top of the cutter head is flush with the top of the second table, and the first table is slightly lower; the cutter head removes a layer of wood equal in the thickness to the difference between the table heights.

A good jointer will give you very smooth, straight surfaces. Particleboard, plywood, laminates, and other manufactured materials are seldom cut on the jointer, however. Their extra hardness and their glues cut poorly, and they quickly dull the cutter.

Planer

Planers are designed to surface wood at a consistent thickness. Like jointers they are not used to surface plywood, particle-board, and laminates. They are usually self-feeding; they move the wood between rollers; and cut from the top surface of the board. Some planers will accept special molding knives.

Planers are sized according to the maximum width and thickness of the stock they will handle. Because modern planers are small enough to be portable, they are included in the dream workshop. These smaller machines, unlike their huge cast-iron predecessors, can be stored in a corner or under the radial arm saw.

Radial Arm Saw

Like the table saw this is an extremely versatile tool. With the proper attachment a radial arm saw will drill, rout, sand, or grind. It can also be used like a saber saw. It costs about the same as a table saw, but it doesn't take up the whole center of the shop. A wall will be fine for the radial arm saw.

The radial arm saw has a base, a worktable, a support column for the arm, and the arm itself, which contains a track on which the motor and saw slide back and forth. When out of use the saw is moved to the rear of the arm, near the support column. Boards to be cut are placed on the table, and the saw is pulled out along the arm to make the cut. A gauge calibrated in degrees located next to the motor is used to align the saw blade. This blade is adjustable on three axes and is capable of a great variety of cutting operations.

The dream shop will include both a table saw and a radial arm saw primarily because the latter will crosscut long pieces of wood that are awkward on the table saw, and the former will rip lumber more efficiently. The table saw is also easier to keep adjusted for making precise cuts.

Band Saw

This popular saw can crosscut, rip, contour along curved lines, resaw wood into thin veneers, and easily accept jigs and fixtures for other tasks. It is the mainstay power tool for boat builders and furniture makers. The band saw gets its name from the long, thin, continuous saw band that runs over two or three wheels and past the saw table. This band is replaceable; it comes with different tooth shapes and different blade widths to meet various requirements. Some band saws have a fence and a miter gauge like the table saw.

Scroll Saw

This is a cousin to the hand-held saber saw. A small floor- or bench-mounted scroll saw will do fine contour work in wood up to 1 inch thick. The blade is removable and can be inserted through a hole drilled in the work to make inside cuts. The newest generation of scroll saws have infinitely variable speeds and parallel arms that tilt the blade back away from the cut on the return stroke for good chip removal. They are also lighter than their earlier counterparts and more suitable for bench mounting or handy storage under a counter.

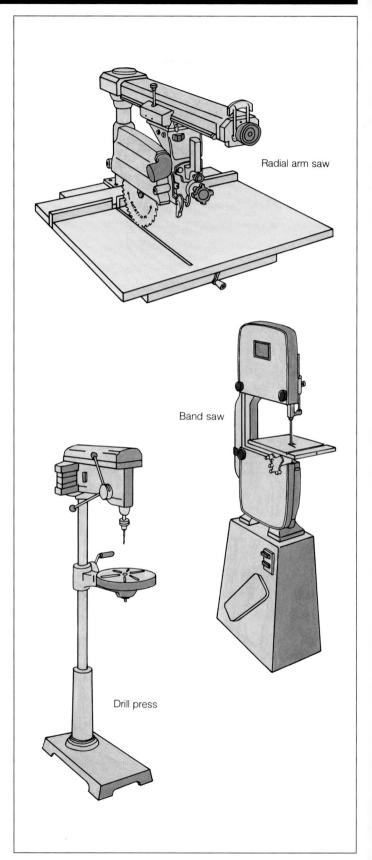

Radial arm saw

Band saw

Drill press

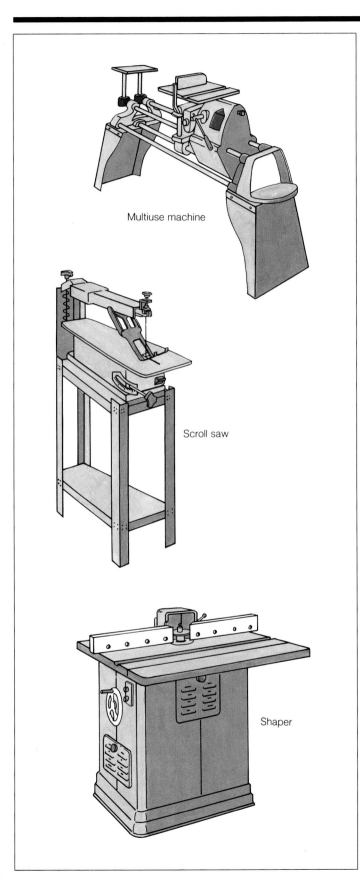

Multiuse machine

Scroll saw

Shaper

Drill Press

It wouldn't be a dream shop without one of these. The drill press will bore accurate holes; with attachments it will also sand, grind, and buff. If you are machining more than one part, it is easy to clamp jigs and fixtures onto the table that will enable you to repeat a given operation. Drill presses are sized by their horsepower, by the distance from the chuck to the column, and by the distance the chuck moves downward in its drilling stroke. In a radial arm drill press, the vertical column is farther away from the chuck to allow wider stock to be put on the table. Drill presses may be purchased in either bench- or floor-mounted models.

Shapers and Routers

These are both high-speed cutting machines. A shaper or router is fitted below a table or to a vertical surface. In the ultimate shop there is one table-mounted unit and one vertical one. Both of these machines enable you to make molding, build a raised-panel door, cut a sliding dovetail, cut recesses for a hinge, and make a rule joint in a table leaf—these are just some of the jobs these machines can do.

Multiuse Machines

For years manufacturers have produced multifunction shop machines. Jointer–table saw units are commonly found on the used-machine market. They usually share the same motor and switch. They take up less floor space than two separate pieces of equipment.

Often a jointer is made in combination with a thickness planer. The jointer table is mounted on the top of the machine. Since it shares the same motor, the same cutter head, and many of the same parts as the planer, it can perform two functions at slightly more than the price of one. This arrangement is also advantageous because it makes for an exceptionally wide jointer. The only disadvantage is that any type of dust control system is more difficult to install.

Some companies produce what is called a five-in-one machine. This type of machine can be converted with relative ease from a table saw to a woodworking lathe to a horizontal boring machine to a disk sander to a drill press. All five are powered by a single motor of high quality. Extra options include a band saw, a belt sander, and a jigsaw. The great advantage of these machines is that they take up no more floor space than a bicycle.

The standard five-in-one machine has a 10-inch variable-speed table saw. This saw can rip 50 inches for large projects and do fine crosscutting, mitering, and beveling. The lathe has a full 34 inches between centers for turning spindles or furniture legs. It will turn up to 16½ inches in diameter. The boring machine will work professional dowelling for doors, cabinets, and other pieces. The 12-inch disk sander is equipped with depth control and variable speed for precision edges, bevels, and joints. The 16½-inch vertical drill press has precision depth control, variable speed, and a full-tilting table.

INDEX

Proof-of-Purchase
0-89721-239-8

U.S./Metric Measure Conversion Chart

		Formulas for Exact Measures			Rounded Measures for Quick Reference		
	Symbol	**When you know:**	**Multiply by:**	**To find:**			
Mass (Weight)	oz	ounces	28.35	grams	1 oz		= 30 g
	lb	pounds	0.45	kilograms	4 oz		= 115 g
	g	grams	0.035	ounces	8 oz		= 225 g
	kg	kilograms	2.2	pounds	16 oz	= 1 lb	= 450 g
					32 oz	= 2 lb	= 900 g
					36 oz	= 2¼ lb	= 1000 g (1 kg)
Volume	tsp	teaspoons	5.0	milliliters	¼ tsp	= 1/24 oz	= 1 ml
	tbsp	tablespoons	15.0	milliliters	½ tsp	= 1/12 oz	= 2 ml
	fl oz	fluid ounces	29.57	milliliters	1 tsp	= 1/6 oz	= 5 ml
	c	cups	0.24	liters	1 tbsp	= ½ oz	= 15 ml
	pt	pints	0.47	liters	1 c	= 8 oz	= 250 ml
	qt	quarts	0.95	liters	2 c (1 pt)	= 16 oz	= 500 ml
	gal	gallons	3.785	liters	4 c (1 qt)	= 32 oz	= 1 liter
	ml	milliliters	0.034	fluid ounces	4 qt (1 gal)	= 128 oz	= 3¾ liter
Length	in.	inches	2.54	centimeters	3/8 in.	= 1 cm	
	ft	feet	30.48	centimeters	1 in.	= 2.5 cm	
	yd	yards	0.9144	meters	2 in.	= 5 cm	
	mi	miles	1.609	kilometers	2½ in.	= 6.5 cm	
	km	kilometers	0.621	miles	12 in. (1 ft)	= 30 cm	
	m	meters	1.094	yards	1 yd	= 90 cm	
	cm	centimeters	0.39	inches	100 ft	= 30 m	
					1 mi	= 1.6 km	
Temperature	° F	Fahrenheit	5/9 (after subtracting 32)	Celsius	32° F	= 0° C	
					68° F	= 20° C	
	° C	Celsius	9/5 (then add 32)	Fahrenheit	212° F	= 100° C	
Area	in.^{2}	square inches	6.452	square centimeters	1 in.^{2}	= 6.5 cm^2	
	ft^2	square feet	929.0	square centimeters	1 ft^2	= 930 cm^2	
	yd^2	square yards	8361.0	square centimeters	1 yd^2	= 8360 cm^2	
	a.	acres	0.4047	hectares	1 a.	= 4050 m^2	